THE COMPLETE SLOW COOKER COOKBOOK for Beginners

Wholesome and Easy British-Inspired Recipes for Breakfast, Lunch, Dinner, Snacks, and Desserts – Perfect for Beginners and Busy Families

Freddie Bowen

Copyright© 2025 By Freddie Bowen

All rights reserved worldwide.

No part of this book may be reproduced or transmitted in any form or by any means, electronic or mechanical, including photo- copying, recording or by any information storage and retrieval system, without written permission from the publisher, except for the inclusion of brief quotations in a review.

Warning-Disclaimer

The purpose of this book is to educate and entertain. The author or publisher does not guarantee that anyone following the techniques, suggestions, tips, ideas, or strategies will become successful. The author and publisher shall have neither liability or responsibility to anyone with respect to any loss or damage caused, or alleged to be caused, directly or indirectly by the information contained in this book.

TABLE OF CONTENTS

1 /	**Introduction**	
4 /	**Chapter 1**	Breakfasts
12 /	**Chapter 2**	Beans and Grains
18 /	**Chapter 3**	Pasta
23 /	**Chapter 4**	Poultry
32 /	**Chapter 5**	Beef, Pork, and Lamb
41 /	**Chapter 6**	Fish and Seafood
52 /	**Chapter 7**	Stews and Soups
62 /	**Chapter 8**	Snacks and Appetizers
69 /	**Chapter 9**	Vegetables and Sides
75 /	**Chapter 10**	Desserts
83 /	**Appendix 1**	Measurement Conversion Chart
84 /	**Appendix 2**	Recipes Index

INTRODUCTION

The Joy of Slow Cooking

Cooking has always been at the heart of family life, but in today's busy world, finding the time to prepare wholesome meals can feel like a challenge. *The Complete Slow Cooker Cookbook for Beginners* was created to show that good food does not need to be complicated or time-consuming. With the gentle power of slow cooking, you can transform simple, affordable ingredients into dishes that are both comforting and nourishing. This approach to cooking not only saves time but also provides consistency and ease, making it perfect for those who are new to the kitchen as well as for busy families who want to enjoy home-cooked meals without stress.

Wholesome Cooking for Everyday Health

One of the greatest advantages of using a slow cooker is its ability to create meals that are deeply flavourful while still supporting a healthy lifestyle. By cooking ingredients slowly, the natural goodness of vegetables, grains, and proteins is preserved, and less oil or additional fats are required. This makes it easier to prepare meals that are lower in unnecessary calories but still satisfying and hearty. *The Complete Slow Cooker Cookbook for Beginners* emphasises wholesome, balanced recipes that are inspired by British traditions, offering both comfort and nutrition in every dish. It is a way of cooking that fits seamlessly into everyday life, aligning with the goal of maintaining energy, wellness, and peace of mind.

Easy Recipes for Beginners and Families

For many people, the thought of cooking can feel intimidating. Complicated instructions, unfamiliar methods, or long lists of ingredients can make home cooking seem out of reach. This cookbook was designed to remove those barriers. Every recipe is written with beginners in mind, with clear steps and simple techniques that ensure success from the very first attempt. Families will also appreciate the straightforward style, as it allows them to prepare meals with minimal effort while still enjoying the rewards of cooking at home. With the slow cooker doing most of the work, there is more time to focus on the things that matter—whether that is spending time with loved ones or simply relaxing after a busy day.

A Practical Way to Live Well

Healthy living is not about extreme changes or difficult routines; it is about finding practical, sustainable habits that support long-term wellness. Cooking with a slow cooker is one of those habits. It reduces the need for constant monitoring, eliminates unnecessary stress in the kitchen, and makes it easier to plan balanced meals. By preparing food in advance and letting it cook slowly, you can ensure that wholesome options are always ready, even on the busiest days. ***The Complete Slow Cooker Cookbook for Beginners*** encourages this balanced approach, showing how cooking can become not only manageable but also enjoyable. The kitchen becomes a place of ease rather than pressure, and meals become an opportunity to nourish both body and spirit.

Inspiration Through Variety

One of the most rewarding aspects of this cookbook is the variety it offers. Covering breakfast, lunch, dinner, snacks, and desserts, it provides a wide range of ideas to suit different tastes, moods, and occasions. Variety is essential to keeping meals exciting and preventing boredom, and the slow cooker makes it possible to create both traditional comfort foods and lighter, health-focused options with equal success. By offering recipes that are inspired by British flavours yet adaptable to personal preferences, this book invites creativity while providing structure. Readers can mix and match dishes across the chapters, creating meal plans that feel both practical and inspiring.

Confidence and Comfort in the Kitchen

At its core, ***The Complete Slow Cooker Cookbook for Beginners*** is about empowerment. It gives readers the confidence to cook at home, to trust in their ability to prepare wholesome meals, and to enjoy the process rather than dread it. The slow cooker is more than an appliance—it is a tool for building confidence, independence, and comfort in the kitchen. Whether you are a complete beginner learning the basics or a busy parent looking for reliable solutions, this book serves as a guide and a companion. It proves that cooking does not need to be complicated to be rewarding. With patience, simplicity, and variety, anyone can create meals that support a healthier, happier lifestyle.

Chapter 1

Breakfasts

Chapter 1 Breakfasts

Bacon-and-Eggs Breakfast Casserole

Prep time: 15 minutes | Cook time: 5 to 6 hours | Serves 8

- 1 tablespoon bacon fat or extra-virgin olive oil
- 12 eggs
- 1 cup coconut milk
- 1 pound (454 g) bacon, chopped and cooked crisp
- ½ sweet onion, chopped
- 2 teaspoons minced garlic
- ¼ teaspoon freshly ground black pepper
- ⅛ teaspoon salt
- Pinch red pepper flakes

1. Grease the slow-cooker insert lightly with either bacon fat or olive oil.
2. In a medium-sized bowl, whisk the eggs with coconut milk, bacon, onion, garlic, pepper, salt, and red pepper flakes until well combined. Pour the mixture into the prepared insert.
3. Place the lid on and cook on low heat for 5 to 6 hours.
4. Serve hot straight from the slow cooker.

Coconut Butter Bread

Prep time: 10 minutes | Cook time: 3 to 4 hours | Makes 8 slices

- 1 tablespoon butter, softened
- 6 large eggs
- ½ cup coconut oil, melted
- 1 teaspoon pure vanilla extract
- ¼ teaspoon liquid stevia
- 1 cup almond flour
- ½ cup coconut flour
- 1 ounce (28 g) protein powder
- 1 teaspoon baking powder

1. Grease an 8-by-4-inch loaf pan with the butter.
2. In a medium bowl, whisk together the eggs, oil, vanilla, and stevia until well blended.
3. In a small bowl, stir together the almond flour, coconut flour, protein powder, and baking powder until mixed.
4. Add the dry ingredients to the wet ingredients and stir to combine.
5. Spoon the batter into the loaf pan and place the loaf pan on a rack in the slow cooker.
6. Cover and cook on low for 3 to 4 hours, until a knife inserted in the center comes out clean.
7. Cool the bread in the loaf pan for 15 minutes. Then remove the bread from the pan and place onto a wire rack to cool completely.
8. Store in a sealed container in the refrigerator for up to 1 week.

Streusel Cake

Prep time: 10 minutes | Cook time: 3 to 4 hours | Serves 8 to 10

- 1 (16-ounce / 454-g) package pound cake mix, prepared according to package directions
- ¼ cup packed brown sugar
- 1 tablespoon flour
- ¼ cup chopped nuts
- 1 teaspoon cinnamon

1. Generously grease and flour a 2-pound (907-g) coffee can or a slow cooker baking insert that fits inside the cooker, then pour in the prepared cake mix.
2. In a separate small bowl, combine the brown sugar, flour, nuts, and cinnamon, and sprinkle this mixture evenly over the cake batter.
3. Place the coffee can or baking insert into the slow cooker, then cover the top with several layers of paper towels.
4. Put the lid on the slow cooker and cook on high for 3 to 4 hours, or until a toothpick inserted into the center of the cake comes out clean.
5. Take the baking tin out of the slow cooker and let it rest for 30 minutes before slicing into wedges to serve.

Breakfast Fruit Compote

Prep time: 5 minutes | Cook time: 2 to 7 hours | Serves 8 to 9

- 1 (12-ounce / 340-g) package dried apricots
- 1 (12-ounce / 340-g) package pitted dried plums
- 1 (11-ounce / 312-g) can mandarin oranges in light syrup, undrained
- 1 (29-ounce / 822-g) can sliced peaches in light syrup, undrained
- ¼ cup white raisins
- 10 maraschino cherries

1. Place all the ingredients into the slow cooker and stir until everything is evenly blended.
2. Secure the lid and cook either on low for 6 to 7 hours or switch to high and cook for 2 to 3 hours.

Pumpkin Pudding with Nutmeg

Prep time: 15 minutes | Cook time: 6 to 7 hours | Serves 8

- ¼ cup melted butter, divided
- 2½ cups canned pumpkin purée
- 2 cups coconut milk
- 4 eggs
- 1 tablespoon pure vanilla extract
- 1 cup almond flour
- ½ cup granulated erythritol
- 2 ounces (57 g) protein powder
- 1 teaspoon baking powder
- 1 teaspoon ground cinnamon
- ¼ teaspoon ground nutmeg
- Pinch ground cloves

1. Lightly grease the insert of the slow cooker with 1 tablespoon of the butter.
2. In a large bowl, whisk together the remaining butter, pumpkin, coconut milk, eggs, and vanilla until well blended.
3. In a small bowl, stir together the almond flour, erythritol, protein powder, baking powder, cinnamon, nutmeg, and cloves.
4. Add the dry ingredients to the wet ingredients and stir to combine.
5. Pour the mixture into the insert.
6. Cover and cook on low for 6 to 7 hours.
7. Serve warm.

Sausage and Hash-Brown Casserole

Prep time: 25 minutes | Cook time: 2½ to 3 hours | Serves 8

- 1½ pounds (680 g) bulk pork sausage
- 2 medium onions, finely chopped
- 1 Anaheim chile, cored, seeded and finely chopped
- 1 medium red bell pepper, seeded and finely chopped
- 1 teaspoon ground cumin
- ½ teaspoon dried oregano
- 1 (16-ounce / 454-g) package frozen shredded hash brown potatoes, defrosted, or 2 cups fresh shredded hash browns
- 6 large eggs, beaten
- 1 cup milk
- 1 cup mayonnaise
- 1 cup prepared salsa (your choice of heat)
- 2 cups shredded mild Cheddar cheese, or 1 cup shredded mild Cheddar mixed with 1 cup shredded Pepper Jack cheese

1. Lightly coat the insert of a 5- to 7-quart slow cooker with nonstick spray, or line it with a slow-cooker liner as directed by the manufacturer.
2. In a large skillet set over high heat, brown the sausage until it loses its pink colour, breaking it apart with the edge of a spoon as it cooks.
3. Drain off all but 1 tablespoon of the fat, then return the skillet to medium-high heat. Add the onions, chile, bell pepper, cumin, and oregano, cooking and stirring until the onions turn soft and translucent, about 5 to 6 minutes. Transfer this mixture to a bowl to cool.
4. Stir the potatoes into the cooled mixture. In another bowl, whisk the eggs, milk, and mayonnaise until smooth, then pour over the sausage and potato mixture and mix well.
5. Spoon half of this mixture into the prepared slow-cooker insert, layering with half the salsa and half the cheese. Repeat the process with the rest of the ingredients. Cover and cook on high for 2½ to 3 hours, until the casserole is puffed and set, reaching 170ºF / 77ºC on an instant-read thermometer. Remove the lid and let the frittata stand for 30 minutes.
6. Serve directly from the cooker on the warm setting.

Breakfast Risotto with Sausage

Prep time: 20 minutes | Cook time: 7 hours | Serves 2

- 8 ounces (227 g) pork sausage
- 1 onion, chopped
- 2 garlic cloves, minced
- Nonstick cooking spray
- 1 cup sliced cremini mushrooms
- 1 cup Arborio rice
- 3 cups chicken stock
- ½ cup milk
- ½ teaspoon salt
- ½ teaspoon dried marjoram leaves
- ⅛ teaspoon freshly ground black pepper
- ⅓ cup grated Parmesan cheese
- 1 tablespoon butter

1. In a medium saucepan over medium heat, cook the sausage, onion, and garlic until the sausage is browned, about 10 minutes, stirring to break up the meat. Drain well.
2. Spray the slow cooker with the nonstick cooking spray.
3. In the slow cooker, combine the sausage mixture, mushrooms, and rice. Add the stock, milk, salt, marjoram, and pepper, and stir.
4. Cover and cook on low for 7 hours.
5. Stir in the cheese and butter. Let stand for 5 minutes, and then serve.

Oatmeal with Nuts

Prep time: 10 minutes | Cook time: 7 hours | Makes 7 cups

- 1 cup chopped walnuts
- Nonstick cooking spray
- 2 cups rolled oats (not instant or quick cooking)
- 1 cup raisins
- 3 cups almond milk
- 1½ cups apple juice
- ⅓ cup honey
- ⅓ cup brown sugar
- ½ teaspoon ground cinnamon
- ¼ teaspoon ground nutmeg
- ¼ teaspoon salt

1. In a small saucepan over medium-low heat, toast the walnuts until fragrant, about 2 minutes, stirring frequently.
2. Spray the slow cooker with the nonstick cooking spray.
3. In the slow cooker, combine the walnuts, oats, and raisins.
4. In a large bowl, beat the almond milk, apple juice, honey, brown sugar, cinnamon, nutmeg, and salt. Pour the mixture into the slow cooker.
5. Cover and cook on low for 7 hours, or until the oatmeal is thickened and tender, and serve.

Baked-Style Oatmeal

Prep time: 10 minutes | Cook time: 2½ to 3 hours | Serves 4 to 6

- ⅓ cup oil
- ½ cup sugar
- 1 large egg, beaten
- 2 cups dry quick oats
- 1½ teaspoons baking powder
- ½ teaspoon salt
- ¾ cup milk

1. Pour the oil into the slow cooker to grease bottom and sides.
2. Add remaining ingredients. Mix well.
3. Cook on low 20 to 30 minutes.

Huevos Rancheros

Prep time: 10 minutes | Cook time: 3 hours | Serves 8

- 1 tablespoon extra-virgin olive oil
- 10 eggs
- 1 cup heavy (whipping) cream
- 1 cup shredded Monterey Jack cheese, divided
- 1 cup prepared or homemade salsa
- 1 scallion, green and white parts, chopped
- 1 jalapeño pepper, chopped
- ½ teaspoon chili powder
- ½ teaspoon salt
- 1 avocado, chopped, for garnish
- 1 tablespoon chopped cilantro, for garnish

1. Use the olive oil to lightly coat the insert of the slow cooker.
2. In a mixing bowl, whisk the eggs with the heavy cream, ½ cup cheese, salsa, scallion, jalapeño, chili powder, and salt until well blended. Pour this mixture into the prepared insert and scatter the remaining ½ cup cheese evenly over the top.
3. Cover with the lid and cook on low for about 3 hours, or until the eggs have set firmly.
4. Allow the eggs to cool just a bit, then slice into wedges and serve with avocado and cilantro as garnish.

Vegetable Omelet

Prep time: 15 minutes | Cook time: 4 to 5 hours | Serves 8

- 1 tablespoon extra-virgin olive oil
- 10 eggs
- ½ cup heavy (whipping) cream
- 1 teaspoon minced garlic
- ¼ teaspoon salt
- ⅛ teaspoon freshly ground black pepper
- ½ cup chopped cauliflower
- ½ cup chopped broccoli
- 1 red bell pepper, chopped
- 1 scallion, white and green parts, chopped
- 4 ounces (113 g) goat cheese, crumbled
- 2 tablespoons chopped parsley, for garnish

1. Brush the slow-cooker insert lightly with olive oil to grease it.
2. In a medium bowl, whisk the eggs, heavy cream, garlic, salt, and pepper until smooth. Fold in the cauliflower, broccoli, red bell pepper, and scallion. Transfer this mixture to the slow cooker and scatter goat cheese across the top.
3. Cover with the lid and cook on low for 4 to 5 hours.
4. Serve warm, garnished with parsley on top.

Strata with Salmon and Dill

Prep time: 20 minutes | Cook time: 4½ hours | Serves 6 to 8

- 6 large eggs
- 1 cup whole or low-fat milk
- 1 cup sour cream (low fat is okay), plus additional for serving
- 3 cups cooked salmon in chunks
- ¼ cup chopped fresh dill
- ¼ cup finely chopped red onion
- 2 teaspoons grated lemon zest
- ½ teaspoon freshly ground white pepper
- 6 plain or egg bagels, cut into ½-inch pieces
- 1 (8-ounce / 227-g) package cream cheese, cut into ½-inch cubes
- ½ cup drained and chopped capers for serving
- Lemon wedges for serving

1. Coat the insert of a 5- to 7-quart slow cooker with nonstick cooking spray or line the insert with a slow-cooker liner according the manufacturer's directions.
2. Whisk together the eggs, milk, and sour cream in a large mixing bowl until smooth. Fold in the salmon, dill, onion, lemon zest, and pepper. Add the bagel pieces and mix, saturating the bread.
3. Transfer half the mixture to the slow cooker and dot with half the cream cheese cubes. Repeat the layers. Cover and cook on low for 4 hours, until the strata is cooked through (170ºF / 77ºC on an instant-read thermometer). Remove the lid and cook for an additional 30 minutes.
4. Serve the strata from the cooker set on warm with the additional sour cream, capers, and the lemon wedges on the side.

Overnight Soaked Oatmeal

Prep time: 5 minutes | Cook time: 3 to 10 hours | Serves 8

- 3¾ cups old-fashioned rolled oats
- 8 cups water
- ½ teaspoon salt
- 4 tablespoons (½ stick) unsalted butter, cut into small pieces
- 2 cups milk or cream, warmed, for serving
- ¼ cup cinnamon sugar for serving

1. Coat the insert of a 5- to 7-quart slow cooker with nonstick cooking spray or line the insert with a slow-cooker liner according to manufacturer's directions.
2. Combine the oatmeal, water, and salt in the cooker. Cover and cook on low for 8 to 10 hours or on high for 3 to 4 hours, until the oats are creamy. Stir in the butter.
3. Serve with warmed milk and cinnamon sugar.

Breakfast Wassail

Prep time: 5 minutes | Cook time: 3 hours | Makes 4 quarts

- 1 (64-ounce / 1.8-kg) bottle cranberry juice
- 1 (32-ounce / 907-g) bottle apple juice
- 1 (12-ounce / 340-g) can frozen pineapple juice concentrate
- 1 (12-ounce / 340-g) can frozen lemonade concentrate
- 3 to 4 cinnamon sticks
- 1 quart water (optional)

1. Place all the ingredients except the water into the slow cooker. If the mixture tastes overly sweet, stir in some water.
2. Put the lid on and cook on low for 3 hours.

Pumpkin Pecan N'Oatmeal Bowl

Prep time: 10 minutes | Cook time: 8 hours | Serves 4

- 1 tablespoon coconut oil
- 3 cups cubed pumpkin, cut into 1-inch chunks
- 2 cups coconut milk
- ½ cup ground pecans
- 1 ounce (28 g) plain protein powder
- 2 tablespoons granulated erythritol
- 1 teaspoon maple extract
- ½ teaspoon ground nutmeg
- ¼ teaspoon ground cinnamon
- Pinch ground allspice

1. Lightly grease the insert of a slower cooker with the coconut oil.
2. Place the pumpkin, coconut milk, pecans, protein powder, erythritol, maple extract, nutmeg, cinnamon, and allspice in the insert.
3. Cover and cook on low for 8 hours.
4. Stir the mixture or use a potato masher to create your preferred texture, and serve.

Southwest Breakfast Casserole

Prep time: 10 minutes | Cook time: 8 hours | Serves 2

- 1 teaspoon butter, at room temperature, or extra-virgin olive oil
- 2 eggs
- 2 egg whites
- 1 teaspoon ground cumin
- 1 teaspoon smoked paprika
- ⅛ teaspoon sea salt
- Freshly ground black pepper
- ½ cup shredded pepper Jack cheese
- ½ cup canned fire-roasted diced tomatoes
- ½ cup canned black beans, drained and rinsed
- 1 teaspoon minced garlic
- 3 corn tortillas
- ¼ cup fresh cilantro, for garnish

1. Rub the inside of the slow cooker with butter to grease it.
2. In a small bowl, whisk together the eggs, egg whites, cumin, paprika, salt, and a few twists of black pepper.
3. In another small bowl, mix the cheese, tomatoes, black beans, and garlic until combined.
4. Lay one corn tortilla on the bottom of the slow cooker. Spread half of the cheese and bean mixture on top, then pour one-third of the egg mixture over it. Add another tortilla and repeat with the remaining cheese mixture plus another third of the egg mixture. Place the final tortilla on top and pour the rest of the egg mixture over it.
5. Cover with the lid and cook on low for 8 hours or overnight. Sprinkle with fresh cilantro before serving.

Warm Wheat Berry Cereal

Prep time: 5 minutes | Cook time: 10 hours | Serves 4

- 1 cup wheat berries
- 5 cups water

1. Rinse and sort berries. Cover with water and soak all day (or 8 hours) in slow cooker.
2. Cover. Cook on low overnight (or 10 hours).
3. Drain, if needed. Serve.

Polenta

Prep time: 10 minutes | Cook time: 2 to 9 hours | Serves 8 to 10

- 4 tablespoons melted butter, divided
- ¼ teaspoon paprika
- 6 cups boiling water
- 2 cups dry cornmeal
- 2 teaspoons salt

1. Use 1 tablespoon of butter to grease the inside of the slow cooker lightly, then sprinkle with paprika. Set the cooker to high.
2. Add the rest of the ingredients to the slow cooker in the order given, including the additional 1 tablespoon butter, and stir until combined.
3. Cover and cook on high for 2 to 3 hours, or on low for 6 to 9 hours, stirring from time to time.
4. Transfer the hot polenta into 2 greased loaf pans and refrigerate for at least 8 hours or overnight.
5. When ready to serve, slice into ¼-inch-thick pieces. Melt 2 tablespoons of butter in a large nonstick skillet, add the slices, and cook until golden on one side, then flip to brown the other side.
6. For a breakfast option, serve with your preferred sweetener.

Broccoli Cornbread Bake

Prep time: 15 minutes | Cook time: 6 hours | Serves 8

- 1 stick butter, melted
- 1 (10-ounce / 283-g) package chopped broccoli, cooked and drained
- 1 onion, chopped
- 1 box cornbread mix
- 4 eggs, well beaten
- 8 ounces (227 g) cottage cheese
- 1¼ teaspoons salt

1. Combine all ingredients. Mix well.
2. Pour into greased slow cooker. Cook on low 6 hours, or until toothpick inserted in center comes out clean.
3. Serve like spoon bread, or invert the pot, remove bread, and cut into wedges.

Cottage Cheese Bread

Prep time: 5 minutes | Cook time: 2 hours | Serves 8

- 1 cup fat-free cottage cheese
- 4 egg whites
- 1 cup sugar
- ¾ cup fat-free or 2% milk
- 1 teaspoon vanilla
- 2¾ cups reduced-fat buttermilk baking mix
- ½ cup raisins or dried cranberries
- ½ teaspoon orange zest

1. Place all the ingredients into a mixing bowl and stir until evenly combined.
2. Transfer the mixture into a greased slow cooker insert.
3. Cover with the lid and cook on high for 2 hours.

Apple Overnight Oatmeal

Prep time: 10 minutes | Cook time: 6 to 8 hours | Serves 4

- 2 cups skim or 2% milk
- 2 tablespoons honey, or ¼ cup brown sugar
- 1 tablespoon margarine
- ¼ teaspoon salt
- ½ teaspoon ground cinnamon
- 1 cup dry rolled oats
- 1 cup apples, chopped
- ½ cup raisins (optional)
- ¼ cup walnuts, chopped
- ½ cup fat-free half-and-half

1. Spray inside of slow cooker with nonfat cooking spray.
2. In a mixing bowl, combine all ingredients except half-and-half. Pour into cooker.
3. Cover and cook on low overnight, ideally 6 to 8 hours. The oatmeal is ready to eat in the morning.
4. Stir in the half-and-half just before serving.

Blueberry Delight

Prep time: 15 minutes | Cook time: 3 to 4 hours | Serves 12

- 1 loaf Italian bread, cubed, divided
- 1 pint blueberries, divided
- 8 ounces (227 g) cream cheese, cubed, divided
- 6 eggs
- 1½ cups milk

1. Place half the bread cubes in the slow cooker.
2. Drop half the blueberries over top the bread.
3. Sprinkle half the cream cheese cubes over the blueberries.
4. Repeat all 3 layers.
5. In a mixing bowl, whisk together eggs and milk. Pour over all ingredients.
6. Cover and cook on low until the dish is set.
7. Serve.

Slow Cooked Fruited Oatmeal with Nuts

Prep time: 15 minutes | Cook time: 6 hours | Serves 6

- 3 cups water
- 2 cups old-fashioned oats
- 2 cups chopped apples
- 1 cup dried cranberries
- 1 cup fat-free milk
- 2 teaspoons butter, melted
- 1 teaspoon pumpkin pie spice
- 1 teaspoon ground cinnamon
- 6 tablespoons chopped almonds, toasted
- 6 tablespoons chopped pecans, toasted
- Additional fat-free milk

1. Spray a 3-quart slow cooker with cooking spray, then add the first eight ingredients. Cover and cook on low for 6 to 8 hours, until the liquid has been absorbed.
2. Ladle the oatmeal into bowls, topping with almonds and pecans. If you like, drizzle a little extra milk over each serving.

Carrot Cake-Inspired Oatmeal

Prep time: 10 minutes | Cook time: 6 hours | Serves 8

- 4½ cups water
- 1 (20-ounce / 567-g) can crushed pineapple, undrained
- 2 cups shredded carrots
- 1 cup steel-cut oats
- 1 cup raisins
- 2 teaspoons ground cinnamon
- 1 teaspoon pumpkin pie spice
- Brown sugar (optional)

1. In a 4-quart slow cooker coated with cooking spray, combine the first seven ingredients. Cover and cook on low for 6 to 8 hours or until oats are tender and liquid is absorbed. Sprinkle with brown sugar if desired.

Spanakopita Frittata

Prep time: 10 minutes | Cook time: 5 to 6 hours | Serves 8

- 1 tablespoon extra-virgin olive oil
- 12 eggs
- 1 cup heavy (whipping) cream
- 2 teaspoons minced garlic
- 2 cups chopped spinach
- ½ cup feta cheese
- Cherry tomatoes, halved, for garnish (optional)
- yoghurt, for garnish (optional)
- Parsley, for garnish (optional)

1. Use olive oil to lightly coat the insert of the slow cooker.
2. In a medium-sized bowl, whisk the eggs, heavy cream, garlic, spinach, and feta until well combined. Pour this mixture into the prepared insert.
3. Cover with the lid and cook on low for 5 to 6 hours.
4. Serve warm, garnished with tomatoes, a spoonful of yoghurt, and parsley if you like.

Cornbread from Scratch

Prep time: 15 minutes | Cook time: 2 to 3 hours | Serves 6

- 1¼ cups flour
- ¾ cup yellow cornmeal
- ¼ cup sugar
- 4½ teaspoons baking powder
- 1 teaspoon salt
- 1 egg, slightly beaten
- 1 cup milk
- ⅓ cup butter, melted, or oil

1. In a mixing bowl, sift the flour, cornmeal, sugar, baking powder, and salt together, then create a well in the center.
2. Add the egg, milk, and butter into the well and stir gently into the dry mixture until just combined.
3. Transfer the batter into a greased 2-quart mold, cover with a plate, and set the mold on a trivet or rack inside the slow cooker.
4. Cover the cooker and cook on high for 2 to 3 hours.

Chapter 2

Beans and Grains

Chapter 2 Beans and Grains

Calico Beans with Bacon and Beef

Prep time: 20 minutes | Cook time: 2 to 6 hours | Serves 10

- ¼ to ½ pound (227 g) bacon
- 1 pound (454 g) ground beef
- 1 medium onion, chopped
- 1 (2-pound / 907-g) can pork and beans
- 1 (1-pound / 454-g) can Great Northern beans, drained
- 1 (14½-ounce / 411-g) can French-style green beans, drained
- ½ cup brown sugar
- ½ cup ketchup
- ½ teaspoon salt
- 2 tablespoons cider vinegar
- 1 tablespoon prepared mustard

1. Brown bacon, ground beef, and onion in skillet until soft. Drain.
2. Combine all ingredients in slow cooker.
3. Cover Cook on low 5 to 6 hours, or on high 2 to 3 hours.

Slow-Cooked Meaty Jambalaya

Prep time: 25 minutes | Cook time: 7¼ hours | Serves 12

- 1 (28-ounce / 794-g) can diced tomatoes, undrained
- 1 cup reduced-sodium chicken broth
- 1 large green pepper, chopped
- 1 medium onion, chopped
- 2 celery ribs, sliced
- ½ cup white wine or additional reduced-sodium chicken broth
- 4 garlic cloves, minced
- 2 teaspoons Cajun seasoning
- 2 teaspoons dried parsley flakes
- 1 teaspoon dried basil
- 1 teaspoon dried oregano
- ¾ teaspoon salt
- ½ to 1 teaspoon cayenne pepper
- 2 pounds (907 g) boneless skinless chicken thighs, cut into 1-inch pieces
- 1 (12-ounce / 340-g) package fully cooked andouille or other spicy chicken sausage links
- 2 pounds (907 g) uncooked medium shrimp, peeled and deveined
- 8 cups hot cooked brown rice

1. In a large bowl, combine the first 13 ingredients. Place chicken and sausage in a 6-quart slow cooker. Pour tomato mixture over top. Cook, covered, on low 7 to 9 hours or until chicken is tender.
2. Stir in shrimp. Cook, covered, 15 to 20 minutes longer or until shrimp turn pink. Serve with rice.

Easy Baked Beans

Prep time: 10 minutes | Cook time: 2 hours | Serves 8

- 2 (16-ounce / 454-g) cans baked beans
- ¼ cup brown sugar
- ½ teaspoon dried mustard
- ½ cup ketchup
- 2 small onions, chopped
- 1 teaspoon Worcestershire sauce

1. Place all the ingredients into the slow cooker and mix lightly to combine.
2. Secure the lid and cook on high for 2 hours.

Barbecued Lima Beans

Prep time: 10 minutes | Cook time: 8 to 10 hours | Serves 6

- 1¼ cups dried lima beans
- Half a medium onion, chopped in large pieces
- ½ teaspoon salt
- ½ teaspoon dry mustard
- 1 teaspoon cider vinegar
- 2 tablespoons molasses
- ¼ cup chili sauce or medium salsa
- Several drops Tabasco sauce

1. Put the beans in a bowl and cover them with water. Allow them to soak overnight, then drain while saving 1 cup of the soaking liquid.
2. Add all the ingredients to the slow cooker along with the reserved 1 cup of bean liquid.
3. Cover and cook on low for 8 to 10 hours.

Bacon Refried Beans

Prep time: 5 minutes | Cook time: 5 hours | Serves 8

- 2 cups dried red or pinto beans
- 6 cups water
- 2 garlic cloves, minced
- 1 large tomato, peeled, seeded, and chopped, or 1 pint tomato juice
- 1 teaspoon salt
- ½ pound (227 g) bacon
- Shredded cheese

1. Combine beans, water, garlic, tomato, and salt in slow cooker.
2. Cover. Cook on high 5 hours, stirring occasionally. When the beans become soft, drain off some liquid.
3. While the beans cook, brown bacon in skillet. Drain, reserving drippings. Crumble bacon. Add half of bacon and 3 tablespoons drippings to beans. Stir.
4. Mash or purée beans with a food processor. Fry the mashed bean mixture in the remaining bacon drippings. Add more salt to taste.
5. To serve, sprinkle the remaining bacon and shredded cheese on top of beans.

Fruited Wild Rice Pilaf

Prep time: 20 minutes | Cook time: 3½ to 7¾ hours | Serves 8 to 10

- 2 cups wild rice, rinsed with cold water and drained twice
- ½ cup (1 stick) unsalted butter
- 1 medium onion, finely chopped
- 3 stalks celery, finely chopped
- 1 teaspoon dried marjoram
- 4 to 5 cups chicken broth
- ½ cup finely chopped dried apricots
- ½ cup dried cranberries
- ½ teaspoon freshly ground black pepper
- ½ cup sliced almonds, toasted

1. Lightly coat the insert of a 5- to 7-quart slow cooker with nonstick spray, or line it with a slow-cooker liner following the manufacturer's instructions.
2. Place the rice in the slow-cooker insert. In a large skillet over medium-high heat, melt the butter, then add the onion, celery, and marjoram. Sauté for about 4 minutes, or until the vegetables are softened.
3. Transfer the cooked vegetables to the insert. Stir in the broth, apricots, cranberries, and pepper. Cover and cook on high for 2½ to 3 hours, or on low for 7 hours, until the rice becomes tender. Check occasionally to ensure there is enough liquid, adding more broth if necessary. Uncover and continue cooking on low for an additional 30 to 45 minutes. Stir in the almonds before serving.
4. Serve directly from the cooker kept on low.

Scandinavian-Style Beans

Prep time: 50 minutes | Cook time: 8 hours | Serves 8

- 1 pound (454 g) dried pinto beans
- 6 cups water
- 12 ounces (340 g) bacon, or 1 ham hock
- 1 onion, chopped
- 2 to 3 garlic cloves, minced
- ¼ teaspoon pepper
- 1 teaspoon salt
- ¼ cup molasses
- 1 cup ketchup
- Tabasco to taste
- 1 teaspoon Worcestershire sauce
- ¾ cup brown sugar
- ½ cup cider vinegar
- ¼ teaspoon dry mustard

1. Soak beans in water in soup pot for 8 hours. Bring beans to boil and cook 1½ to 2 hours, or until soft. Drain, reserving liquid.
2. Combine all ingredients in slow cooker, using just enough bean liquid to cover everything. Cook on low 5 to 6 hours. If using ham hock, debone, cut ham into bite-sized pieces, and mix into beans.

No-Meat Baked Beans

Prep time: 10 minutes | Cook time: 6½ to 9½ hours | Serves 8 to 10

- 1 pound (454 g) dried navy beans
- 6 cups water
- 1 small onion, chopped
- ¾ cup ketchup
- ½ cup brown sugar
- ¾ cup water
- 1 teaspoon dry mustard
- 3 tablespoons dark molasses
- 1 teaspoon salt

1. Place the beans in a large soup kettle, cover with water, and soak overnight. The next day, cook the beans in fresh water until tender, about 1½ hours, then drain and discard the cooking water.
2. Add the beans and all remaining ingredients to the slow cooker, stirring until everything is thoroughly combined.
3. Cover with the lid and cook on low for 5 to 8 hours, until the beans are flavourful but still hold their shape.

Risi Bisi Pea and Rice

Prep time: 15 minutes | Cook time: 2½ to 3½ hours | Serves 6

- 1½ cups converted long-grain white rice, uncooked
- ¾ cup chopped onions
- 2 garlic cloves, minced
- 2 (14½-ounce / 411-g) cans reduced-sodium chicken broth
- ⅓ cup water
- ¾ teaspoon Italian seasoning
- ½ teaspoon dried basil leaves
- ½ cup frozen baby peas, thawed
- ¼ cup grated Parmesan cheese

1. Combine rice, onions, and garlic in slow cooker.
2. In saucepan, mix together chicken broth and water. Bring to boil. Add Italian seasoning and basil leaves. Stir into rice mixture.
3. Cover. Cook on low 2 to 3 hours, or until liquid is absorbed.
4. Stir in peas. Cover. Cook 30 minutes. Stir in cheese.

Rice and Turkey Slow Cooker Bake

Prep time: 15 minutes | Cook time: 3 to 8 hours | Serves 6

- 1½ pounds (680 g) ground turkey
- 1 teaspoon sea salt
- ½ teaspoon black pepper
- 2 tablespoons chopped fresh thyme
- 2 tablespoons chopped fresh sage
- 2 cups converted brown rice
- 2 cups chicken stock (or turkey stock if you have it)
- 1 tablespoon plus 1 teaspoon balsamic vinegar
- 1 medium yellow onion, chopped
- 2 garlic cloves, minced
- 1 (14-ounce / 397-g) can stewed tomatoes, with the juice
- 3 medium-size zucchini, sliced thinly
- ¼ cup pitted and sliced Kalamata olives
- ¼ cup chopped fresh flat-leaf parsley
- ½ cup grated Parmigiano-Reggiano cheese, for serving (optional)

1. Lightly coat a large skillet with cooking spray and set over medium-high heat. Add the ground turkey along with 1 teaspoon salt, ½ teaspoon pepper, 1 tablespoon thyme, and 1 tablespoon sage. Cook, stirring, until the turkey loses its pink colour. Drain the fat and transfer the mixture to the slow cooker.
2. Stir in the rice, chicken stock, and vinegar. Add the onion, garlic, tomatoes, zucchini, and olives, mixing well. Sprinkle in the remaining 1 tablespoon thyme, the remaining 1 tablespoon sage, and the parsley, then stir until evenly combined.
3. Cover with the lid and cook on low for 6 to 8 hours, or on high for 3 to 4 hours.
4. Taste and adjust seasoning with more salt and pepper if needed. Serve hot, garnished with Parmigiano-Reggiano cheese if desired.

Cajun-Style Beans with Sausage

Prep time: 10 minutes | Cook time: 8 hours | Serves 4 to 6

- 1 pound (454 g) smoked sausage, sliced into ¼-inch pieces
- 1 (16-ounce / 454-g) can red beans
- 1 (16-ounce / 454-g) can crushed tomatoes with green chilies
- 1 cup chopped celery
- Half an onion, chopped
- 2 tablespoons Italian seasoning
- Tabasco sauce to taste

1. Combine all ingredients in slow cooker.
2. Cover. Cook on low 8 hours.
3. Serve.

Auntie Ginny's Classic Baked Beans

Prep time: 15 minutes | Cook time: 4 to 5 hours | Serves 8

- 4 slices bacon, diced
- 1 (28-ounce / 794-g) can pork and beans
- 1 teaspoon dark molasses
- 1 tablespoon brown sugar
- 1 cup dates, cut up
- 1 medium onion, chopped

1. Partially fry bacon. Drain.
2. Combine ingredients in slow cooker.
3. Cover. Cook on low 4 to 5 hours.

Rice 'n Beans 'n Salsa

Prep time: 10 minutes | Cook time: 4 to 10 hours | Serves 6 to 8

- 2 (16-ounce / 454-g) cans black or navy beans, drained
- 1 (14-ounce / 397-g) chicken broth
- 1 cup long-grain white or brown rice, uncooked
- 1 quart salsa, your choice of heat
- 1 cup water
- ½ teaspoon garlic powder

1. Place all the ingredients into the slow cooker and mix thoroughly to combine.
2. Cover with the lid and cook on low for 8 to 10 hours, or set to high and cook for 4 hours.

From-Scratch Baked Beans

Prep time: 10 minutes | Cook time: 14 hours | Serves 6

- 2½ cups Great Northern dried beans
- 4 cups water
- 1½ cups tomato sauce
- ½ cup brown sugar
- 2 teaspoons salt
- 1 small onion, chopped
- ½ teaspoon chili powder

1. Rinse the dry beans thoroughly and drain. Place the beans and water in the slow cooker and cook on low for 8 hours or overnight.
2. Add the rest of the ingredients, stirring to combine. Continue cooking on low for 6 more hours. If the beans seem too watery toward the end, remove the lid for the last 30 to 60 minutes.

Cheddar Cheese Rice

Prep time: 15 minutes | Cook time: 2 to 3 hours | Serves 8 to 10

- 2 cups brown rice, uncooked
- 3 tablespoons butter
- ½ cup thinly sliced green onions or shallots
- 1 teaspoon salt
- 5 cups water
- ½ teaspoon pepper
- 2 cups shredded Cheddar cheese
- 1 cup slivered almonds (optional)

1. Combine rice, butter, green onion, and salt in slow cooker.
2. Bring water to boil and pour over rice mixture.
3. Cover and cook on high 2 to 3 hours, or until rice is tender and liquid is absorbed.
4. Five minutes before serving stir in pepper and cheese.
5. Garnish with slivered almonds, if you wish

Mixed Slow Cooker Beans

Prep time: 10 minutes | Cook time: 4 to 5 hours | Serves 6

- 1 (16-ounce / 454-g) can kidney beans, drained
- 1 (15½-ounce / 439-g) can baked beans, undrained
- 1 pint home-frozen, or 1 (1-pound / 454-g) package frozen, lima beans
- 1 pint home-frozen, or 1 (1-pound / 454-g) package frozen, green beans
- 4 slices lean turkey bacon, browned and crumbled
- ½ cup ketchup
- ⅓ cup sugar
- ⅓ cup brown sugar
- 2 tablespoons vinegar
- ½ teaspoon salt

1. Place the beans and bacon into the slow cooker.
2. In a separate bowl, mix the remaining ingredients together, then add them to the beans and stir until well combined.
3. Cover with the lid and cook on low for 4 to 5 hours.

Slow Cooker Kidney Beans

Prep time: 15 minutes | Cook time: 6 to 7 hours | Serves 12

- 2 (30-ounce / 850-g) cans kidney beans, rinsed and drained
- 1 (28-ounce / 794-g) can diced tomatoes, drained
- 2 medium red bell peppers, chopped
- 1 cup ketchup
- ½ cup brown sugar
- ¼ cup honey
- ¼ cup molasses
- 1 tablespoon Worcestershire sauce
- 1 teaspoon dry mustard
- 2 medium red apples, cored, cut into pieces

1. Place all the ingredients except the apples into the slow cooker and mix well.
2. Cover with the lid and cook on low for 4 to 5 hours.
3. Add the apples and stir them into the mixture.
4. Replace the lid and continue cooking for another 2 hours.

Classic Wild Rice Pilaf

Prep time: 10 minutes | Cook time: 3½ to 5 hours | Serves 6

- 1½ cups wild rice, uncooked
- ½ cup finely chopped onion
- 1 (14-ounce / 397-g) chicken broth
- 2 cups water
- 1 (4-ounce / 113-g) can sliced mushrooms, drained
- ½ teaspoon dried thyme leaves
- Nonstick cooking spray

1. Spray slow cooker with nonstick cooking spray.
2. Rinse rice and drain well.
3. Combine rice, onion, chicken broth, and water in slow cooker. Mix well.
4. Cover and cook on high 3 to 4 hours.
5. Add mushrooms and thyme and stir gently.
6. Cover and cook on low 30 to 60 minutes longer, or until wild rice pops and is tender.

Vegetarian Chili in Slow Cooker

Prep time: 15 minutes | Cook time: 4 to 8 hours | Serves 4

- 1 (28-ounce / 794-g) can chopped whole tomatoes, with the juice
- 1 medium green bell pepper, chopped
- 1 (15-ounce / 425-g) can red beans, drained and rinsed
- 1 (15-ounce / 425-g) can black beans, drained and rinsed
- 1 yellow onion, chopped
- 1 tablespoon olive oil
- 1 tablespoon onion powder
- 1 teaspoon garlic powder
- 1 teaspoon cayenne pepper
- 1 teaspoon paprika
- ½ teaspoon sea salt
- ½ teaspoon black pepper
- 1 large Hass avocado, pitted, peeled, and chopped, for garnish

1. Combine the tomatoes, bell pepper, red beans, black beans, and onion in the slow cooker. Sprinkle with the onion powder, garlic powder, cayenne pepper, paprika, ½ teaspoon salt, and ½ teaspoon black pepper.
2. Cover and cook on high for 4 to 6 hours or on low for 8 hours, or until thick.
3. Season with salt and black pepper if needed. Served hot, garnished with some of the avocado.

Chili Boston Baked Beans

Prep time: 15 minutes | Cook time: 6 to 8 hours | Serves 20

- 1 cup raisins
- 2 small onions, diced
- 2 tart apples, diced
- 1 cup chili sauce
- 1 cup chopped ham or crumbled bacon
- 2 (15-ounce / 425-g) cans baked beans
- 3 teaspoons dry mustard
- ½ cup sweet pickle relish

1. Combine all the ingredients in a bowl and stir until well blended.
2. Transfer to the slow cooker, cover, and cook on low for 6 to 8 hours.

Chapter 3

Pasta

Chapter 3 Pasta

Mediterranean Beef Pasta

Prep time: 20 minutes | Cook time: 3 to 9 hours | Serves 6

Basil Gremolata:
- 2 tablespoons finely grated Parmesan cheese
- 2 tablespoons coarsely chopped fresh basil
- 2 cloves garlic, minced

Pasta Dish:
- 1 tablespoon olive oil
- 1½ pounds (680 g) lean beef, cut into 1-inch cubes
- 3 medium carrots, cut into ½-inch slices
- 1 medium yellow or red bell pepper, cut into 1-inch pieces
- 1 medium yellow onion, cut into thin wedges
- 3 cloves garlic, minced
- 1 teaspoon dried oregano
- ½ teaspoon dried rosemary
- ½ teaspoon sea salt
- ¼ teaspoon black pepper
- 1 (15-ounce / 425-g) can diced tomatoes with the juice
- 1 cup beef stock
- 6 ounces (170 g) uncooked whole-grain penne pasta
- 1 medium zucchini, halved lengthwise and cut into ¼-inch slices

Make the Gremolata:

1. In a small bowl, stir together Parmesan, basil, and garlic. Cover and refrigerate while the pasta dish cooks.

Make the Pasta Dish:

2. Heat the olive oil in large skillet over medium-high heat. Add the beef, in two batches, and cook until brown. Drain off the fat.
3. Transfer the beef to the slow cooker. Add the carrots, bell pepper, onion, and garlic. Sprinkle in the oregano, rosemary, salt, and pepper.
4. Pour the tomatoes and beef stock over the mixture. Cover and cook on low for 7 to 9 hours or on high for 3½ to 4½ hours.
5. Add the penne for the last hour of the cooking time.
6. Once the pasta is al dente, if using low heat setting, turn to high heat setting. Stir in the zucchini. Cover and cook for 30 minutes more.
7. Serve hot, sprinkled with the basil gremolata.

Classic Macaroni and Cheese

Prep time: 15 minutes | Cook time: 4½ to 5½ hours | Serves 6 to 8

- 4 tablespoons (½ stick) unsalted butter
- 1 small onion or shallot, finely chopped
- 3 tablespoons all-purpose flour
- 1½ cups chicken broth
- 1½ cups milk
- 4 drops Tabasco sauce
- 5 cups finely shredded mild yellow and sharp white Cheddar cheese, plus extra to top
- 6 cups elbow macaroni, cooked just short of al dente
- ½ cup crushed buttery crackers such as Ritz or Pepperidge Farm Golden Butter Crackers

1. Coat the insert of a 5- to 7-quart slow cooker with nonstick cooking spray or line it with a slow-cooker liner according to the manufacturer's directions.
2. Melt the butter in a saucepan over medium-high heat. Add the onion and sauté until the onion is softened, about 2 minutes. Stir in the flour, and cook for 2 to 3 minutes, whisking constantly. Gradually add the broth and milk and bring the sauce to a boil, whisking constantly.
3. Add the Tabasco and remove the sauce from the heat. Add 3 cups of the cheese to the sauce and stir to melt. Spread half the macaroni in the slow-cooker insert and pour half the sauce over the macaroni.
4. Sprinkle 1 cup of the cheese over the layer. Repeat with the remaining macaroni and sauce and 1 cup of the cheese. Cover and cook for on low for 4 to 5 hours, until the mac and cheese is bubbling and cooked through.
5. Sprinkle a little more cheese and the crackers over the top of the mac and cheese. Remove the cover and cook for an additional 30 minutes. Allow the mac and cheese to rest about 10 minutes.
6. Serve in the cooker set on warm.

Meat-Free Lasagna

Prep time: 15 minutes | Cook time: 5 hours | Serves 8

- 4½ cups fat-free, low-sodium meatless spaghetti sauce
- ½ cup water
- 1 (16-ounce / 454-g) container fat-free ricotta cheese
- 2 cups shredded part-skim Mozzarella cheese, divided
- ¾ cup grated Parmesan cheese, divided
- 1 egg
- 2 teaspoons minced garlic
- 1 teaspoon Italian seasoning
- 1 (8-ounce / 227-g) box no-cook lasagna noodles

1. Stir ½ cup of water into the spaghetti sauce in a bowl until well mixed.
2. In a different bowl, combine the ricotta, 1½ cups Mozzarella, ½ cup Parmesan, the egg, garlic, and seasoning, mixing until smooth.
3. Spread a quarter of the sauce mixture over the bottom of the slow cooker. Lay down a third of the noodles, breaking them if needed so they fit.
4. Cover the noodles with a third of the cheese mixture, making sure no noodle pieces are exposed.
5. Build two more layers in the same order with the remaining ingredients.
6. Finish by spreading the rest of the sauce evenly across the top.
7. Place the lid on the slow cooker and cook on low for 5 hours.
8. Sprinkle the leftover cheeses across the lasagna, re-cover, and let it sit for 10 minutes to allow the cheese to melt before serving.

Herby Slow Cooker Kluski

Prep time: 20 minutes | Cook time: 1 to 2½ hours | Serves 8

- 1 pound (454 g) extra-lean ground beef
- 2 small onions, chopped
- 1 (14-ounce / 397-g) fat-free pizza sauce
- 1 (14-ounce / 397-g) low-fat, low-sodium spaghetti sauce
- 1 teaspoon garlic powder
- 1¼ teaspoons black pepper
- 1 teaspoon dried oregano
- ¼ teaspoon rubbed sage
- 12 ounces (340 g) dry kluski noodles

1. In a nonstick skillet, cook the ground beef with the onions until browned.
2. Either in the skillet or in a large bowl, combine the browned beef and onions with the pizza sauce, spaghetti sauce, and the herbs and seasonings, stirring until blended.
3. Cook the noodles according to the package instructions until tender, then drain well.
4. Spread half of the beef sauce across the bottom of the slow cooker, add the noodles on top, and finish with the rest of the beef sauce.
5. If the ingredients are already hot, cook on low for 1 to 1½ hours. For sauce and noodles at room temperature or just out of the refrigerator, cook on high for 2 to 2½ hours.

Tuna Noodle Casserole

Prep time: 15 minutes | Cook time: 4½ to 5½ hours | Serves 6 to 8

- ½ pound (227 g) wide egg noodles, cooked just short of al dente
- 2 (6-ounce / 170-g) cans solid white albacore tuna packed in oil, drained and broken into chunks
- 4 tablespoons (½ stick) unsalted butter
- 1 small onion, finely chopped (about ¼ cup)
- 2 stalks celery, finely chopped
- 8 ounces (227 g) button mushrooms, sliced
- ¼ cup all-purpose flour
- 3 cups milk
- 4 drops Tabasco sauce
- ½ teaspoon salt
- ½ cup finely crushed potato chips

1. Lightly coat the insert of a 5- to 7-quart slow cooker with nonstick spray, or line it with a slow-cooker liner as directed by the manufacturer.
2. Place the noodles and tuna into the slow-cooker insert and stir to mix. In a large skillet over high heat, melt the butter, then add the onion, celery, and mushrooms. Sauté until most of the liquid evaporates, leaving some fat in the pan.
3. Stir in the flour and cook, stirring constantly, for about 3 minutes. Slowly add the milk, stirring until it comes to a boil. Mix in the Tabasco and salt. Transfer everything from the skillet into the slow-cooker insert.
4. Cover with the lid and cook on low for 4 to 5 hours. Remove the cover, sprinkle the chips over the casserole, then cover again and cook for another 30 minutes.
5. Serve directly from the slow cooker on the warm setting.

Lentil Sauce Pasta

Prep time: 15 minutes | Cook time: 3 to 10 hours | Serves 4 to 6

- ½ cup chopped onions
- ½ cup chopped carrots
- ½ cup chopped celery
- 2 cups diced tomatoes in liquid
- 1 cup tomato sauce
- 3 to 4 ounces (85 to 113 g) dried lentils, rinsed and drained
- ½ teaspoon dried oregano
- ½ teaspoon dried basil
- ½ teaspoon garlic powder
- ¼ teaspoon crushed red pepper flakes
- 4 cups hot angel-hair pasta, cooked

1. Mix all ingredients except pasta in slow cooker.
2. Cover. Cook on low 8 to 10 hours, or on high 3 to 5 hours.
3. Cook pasta according to package directions.
4. Place cooked pasta in large serving bowl and pour lentil sauce over top. Toss to combine.

Cottage Cheese Casserole

Prep time: 20 minutes | Cook time: 4 to 5 hours | Serves 6

- 2½ teaspoons margarine
- ½ cup fresh mushrooms, chopped
- ½ cup onions, chopped
- ½ cup celery, chopped
- 1 clove garlic, minced
- ½ teaspoon dried marjoram
- ¾ cup low-sodium tomato paste
- 4 cups macaroni, cooked
- 1¼ cups water
- 2 teaspoons salt
- 1 teaspoon sugar
- ¼ cup parsley, chopped
- 2 cups low-fat, low-sodium cottage cheese
- ⅓ cup grated Parmesan cheese

1. In a skillet over medium heat, sauté the mushrooms, onions, celery, and garlic in margarine until softened.
2. Mix the sautéed vegetables with the marjoram, tomato paste, macaroni, water, salt, and sugar.
3. Spoon half of the macaroni mixture into the slow cooker.
4. Add a layer of 1 cup cottage cheese, half of the Parmesan cheese, and the parsley.
5. Repeat the layering process with the remaining ingredients.
6. Cover with the lid and cook on high for 4 to 5 hours.

Easy Spaghetti

Prep time: 15 minutes | Cook time: 3¼ to 8¼ hours | Serves 8

- 2 pounds (907 g) ground chuck, browned and drained
- 1 cup chopped onions
- 2 cloves garlic, minced
- 2 (15-ounce / 425-g) cans tomato sauce
- 2 to 3 teaspoons Italian seasoning
- 1½ teaspoons salt
- ¼ teaspoon pepper
- 2 (4-ounce / 113-g) cans sliced mushrooms, drained
- 6 cups tomato juice
- 1 (16-ounce / 454-g) dry spaghetti, broken into 4 to 5-inch pieces
- Grated Parmesan cheese

1. Combine all ingredients except spaghetti and cheese in 4-quart (or larger) slow cooker.
2. Cover. Cook on low 6 to 8 hours, or on high 3 to 5 hours. Turn to high during last 30 minutes and stir in dry spaghetti. (If spaghetti is not fully cooked, continue cooking another 10 minutes, checking to make sure it is not becoming overcooked.)
3. Sprinkle individual servings with Parmesan cheese.

Classic Italian Slow-Simmered Meat Sauce Pasta

Prep time: 20 minutes | Cook time: 6 hours | Serves 6

- 1 pound (454 g) bulk Italian sausage
- 1 medium onion, chopped
- 3 garlic cloves, minced
- 2 (14½-ounce / 411-g) cans diced tomatoes, undrained
- 1 (8-ounce / 227-g) can tomato sauce
- 1 (6-ounce / 170-g) can tomato paste
- 1 tablespoon brown sugar
- 2 bay leaves
- 2 teaspoons dried oregano
- 2 teaspoons dried basil
- 1 teaspoon salt
- ½ teaspoon dried thyme
- ¼ cup minced fresh basil, divided
- Hot cooked pasta

1. In a large skillet, cook sausage and onion over medium heat for 7 to 8 minutes or until sausage is no longer pink and onion is tender. Add garlic; cook 1 minute longer. Drain. Transfer to a 3-quart slow cooker.
2. Stir in the tomatoes, tomato sauce, tomato paste, brown sugar, bay leaves, oregano, dried basil, salt and thyme. Cover and cook on low for 6 to 8 hours.
3. Discard bay leaves; stir in half of the fresh basil. Serve with pasta. Top with remaining basil.

Greek Shrimp Orzo

Prep time: 45 minutes | Cook time: 2 hours | Serves 6

- 2 cups uncooked orzo pasta
- 2 tablespoons minced fresh basil or 2 teaspoons dried basil
- 3 tablespoons olive oil, divided
- 1½ tablespoons chopped shallot
- 2 tablespoons butter
- 1 (14½-ounce / 411-g) can diced tomatoes, drained
- 2 tablespoons minced fresh oregano or 2 teaspoons dried oregano
- 3 garlic cloves, minced
- 1 pound (454 g) uncooked large shrimp, peeled and deveined
- 1 cup oil-packed sun-dried tomatoes, chopped
- 2½ cups crumbled feta cheese
- 1½ cups pitted Greek olives

1. Prepare the orzo as directed on the package, then rinse under cold water and drain thoroughly. Place it in a large bowl, drizzle with 1 tablespoon of oil, add the basil, and toss well to coat. Set the mixture aside.
2. Melt the butter with the remaining oil in a large skillet and sauté the shallot until soft. Add the garlic, oregano, and diced tomatoes, stirring and cooking for 1 to 2 minutes. Next, add the shrimp and sun-dried tomatoes, continuing to stir for 2 to 3 minutes, or until the shrimp have turned pink.
3. Spoon the mixture into a greased 5-quart slow cooker. Add the orzo mixture along with the cheese and olives, stirring everything together. Cover and cook on low for 2 to 3 hours, or until warmed through.

Chapter 4

Poultry

Chapter 4 Poultry

Chicken Stew Italian Style

Prep time: 20 minutes | Cook time: 3 to 6 hours | Serves 4

- 2 boneless, skinless chicken breast halves, uncooked, cut in 1½-inch pieces
- 1 (19-ounce / 539-g) can cannellini beans, drained and rinsed
- 1 (15½-ounce / 439-g) can kidney beans, drained and rinsed
- 1 (14½-ounce / 411-g) can low-sodium diced tomatoes, undrained
- 1 cup chopped celery
- 1 cup sliced carrots
- 2 small garlic cloves, coarsely chopped
- 1 cup water
- ½ cup dry red wine or low-fat chicken broth
- 3 tablespoons tomato paste
- 1 tablespoon sugar
- 1½ teaspoons dried Italian seasoning

1. Combine chicken, cannellini beans, kidney beans, tomatoes, celery, carrots, and garlic in slow cooker. Mix well.
2. In medium bowl, combine all remaining ingredients. Mix well. Pour over chicken and vegetables. Mix well.
3. Cover. Cook on low 5 to 6 hours, or on high 3 hours.

Braised Chicken Thighs with Garlic

Prep time: 15 minutes | Cook time: 7 to 8 hours | Serves 4

- ¼ cup extra-virgin olive oil, divided
- 1½ pounds (680 g) boneless chicken thighs
- 1 teaspoon paprika
- Salt, for seasoning
- Freshly ground black pepper, for seasoning
- 1 sweet onion, chopped
- 4 garlic cloves, thinly sliced
- ½ cup chicken broth
- 2 tablespoons freshly squeezed lemon juice
- ½ cup Greek yoghurt

1. Lightly grease the insert of the slow cooker with 1 tablespoon of the olive oil.
2. Season the thighs with paprika, salt, and pepper.
3. In a large skillet over medium-high heat, heat the remaining olive oil. Add the chicken and brown for 5 minutes, turning once.
4. Transfer the chicken to the insert and add the onion, garlic, broth, and lemon juice.
5. Cover and cook on low for 7 to 8 hours.
6. Stir in the yoghurt and serve.

Cumin-Spiced Chicken Wings

Prep time: 10 minutes | Cook time: 4 to 6 hours | Serves 6

- 3 tablespoons rapeseed oil
- 2 teaspoons ground cumin seeds, ground
- 2 teaspoons crushed garlic
- 2 teaspoons freshly grated ginger
- 1 teaspoon cumin seeds
- 1 teaspoon salt
- 1 teaspoon coriander seeds, ground
- 1 teaspoon chili powder
- 2 fresh green chiles, finely sliced
- 24 chicken wings
- Handful fresh coriander leaves, chopped
- Juice of 1 lemon
- 1 teaspoon red chili flakes (optional)

1. Turn the slow cooker on high to preheat.
2. In a bowl, combine all the ingredients except the coriander leaves, lemon juice, and chili flakes. Add the wings and toss until they are well coated.
3. Arrange the wings in the slow cooker, cover, and cook on low for 6 hours or on high for 4 hours.
4. Before serving, garnish with coriander leaves, a squeeze of lemon juice, and a sprinkle of chili flakes if desired.

Thanksgiving Turkey Breast

Prep time: 20 minutes | Cook time: 3½ to 4 hours | Serves 8

- 2 medium onions, quartered
- 2 medium carrots, cut into 1-inch lengths
- 2 stalks celery, cut into 1-inch lengths
- 2 large sprigs thyme leaves
- 1½ teaspoons salt
- ½ teaspoon freshly ground black pepper
- 1 cup double-strength chicken broth
- 4 strips thick-cut bacon
- 1 (3- to 4-pound / 1.4- to 1.8-kg) bone-in turkey breast
- 2 teaspoons Wondra or other instant blending flour (optional)

1. Arrange the vegetables and thyme in the insert of a 5- to 7-quart slow cooker. Sprinkle with the salt and pepper and pour in the broth.
2. Arrange the bacon on top of the turkey breast and place in the slow-cooker insert on top of the vegetables. Cover and cook on high for 3½ to 4 hours, until the turkey registers 170ºF (77ºC) on an instant-read thermometer. Carefully transfer the turkey breast to a serving platter and discard the bacon.
3. Cover the turkey breast with aluminum foil and allow to rest for 15 minutes. Strain the sauce through a fine-mesh sieve into a saucepan and bring to a boil. Whisk in the flour (if using) and bring back to a boil. Taste and adjust the seasoning. slice the turkey breast and serve with the gravy.

Chicken Gumbo

Prep time: 25 minutes | Cook time: 3 to 10 hours | Serves 6 to 8

- 1 large onion, chopped
- 3 to 4 garlic cloves, minced
- 1 green pepper, diced
- 2 cups okra, sliced
- 2 cups tomatoes, chopped
- 4 cups chicken broth
- 1 pound (454 g) chicken breast, cut into 1-inch pieces
- 2 teaspoons Old Bay Seasoning

1. Place all the ingredients into the slow cooker and stir gently to mix.
2. Cover with the lid and cook on low for 8 to 10 hours, or set to high and cook for 3 to 4 hours.
3. Serve directly from the slow cooker.

Mango Chutney Chicken

Prep time: 10 minutes | Cook time: 6 to 8 hours | Serves 2

- 12 ounces (340 g) boneless, skinless chicken thighs, cut into 1-inch pieces
- ½ cup thinly sliced red onion
- 1 cup canned mango or peaches, drained and diced
- 2 tablespoons golden raisins
- 2 tablespoons apple cider vinegar
- 1 teaspoon minced fresh ginger
- ¼ teaspoon red pepper flakes
- 1 teaspoon curry powder
- ¼ teaspoon ground cinnamon
- ⅛ teaspoon sea salt

1. Put all the ingredients to the slow cooker and gently stir to combine.
2. Cover and cook on low for 6 to 8 hours. The chutney should be thick and sweet and the chicken tender and cooked through.

Reuben Chicken Casserole

Prep time: 30 minutes | Cook time: 4 hours | Serves 6

- 2 (16-ounce / 454-g) cans sauerkraut, rinsed and drained, divided
- 1 cup Light Russian salad dressing, divided
- 6 boneless, skinless chicken breast halves, divided
- 1 tablespoon prepared mustard, divided
- 6 slices Swiss cheese
- Fresh parsley for garnish (optional)

1. Spread half of the sauerkraut in the bottom of the slow cooker and drizzle with ⅓ cup of dressing.
2. Arrange 3 chicken breast halves over the sauerkraut and spread half of the mustard across the chicken.
3. Add the rest of the sauerkraut and place the remaining chicken breasts on top. Drizzle with another ⅓ cup of dressing, reserving the last portion for serving.
4. Cover with the lid and cook on low for 4 hours, or until the chicken is tender but not overcooked.
5. To serve, place one chicken breast half on each plate. Spoon sauerkraut over the chicken, then top with a slice of cheese and drizzle with the reserved dressing. Garnish with parsley if desired, just before serving.

Chicken Curry with Spice

Prep time: 25 minutes | Cook time: 6 to 8 hours | Serves 8

- 4 pounds (1.8 kg) chicken pieces, with bones
- Water
- 2 onions, diced
- 1 (10-ounce / 283-g) package frozen chopped spinach, thawed and squeezed dry
- 1 cup plain yoghurt
- 2 to 3 diced red potatoes
- 3 teaspoons salt
- 1 teaspoon garlic powder
- 1 teaspoon ground ginger
- 1 teaspoon ground cumin
- 1 teaspoon ground coriander
- 1 teaspoon pepper
- 1 teaspoon ground cloves
- 1 teaspoon ground cardamom
- 1 teaspoon ground cinnamon
- ½ teaspoon chili powder
- 1 teaspoon red pepper flakes
- 3 teaspoons turmeric

1. Place chicken in large slow cooker. Cover with water.
2. Cover. Cook on high 2 hours, or until tender.
3. Drain chicken. Remove from slow cooker. Cool briefly and cut/shred into small pieces. Return to slow cooker.
4. Add remaining ingredients.
5. Cover. Cook on low 4 to 6 hours, or until potatoes are tender.
6. Serve.

Orange-Glazed Chicken Breasts

Prep time: 5 minutes | Cook time: 7¼ to 9¼ hours | Serves 6

- 1 (6-ounce / 170-g) can frozen orange juice concentrate, thawed
- ½ teaspoon dried marjoram
- 6 boneless, skinless chicken breast halves
- ¼ cup cold water
- 2 tablespoons cornstarch

1. In a shallow dish, mix the orange juice with the marjoram. Dip each chicken breast into the mixture, then arrange them in the slow cooker. Pour any leftover sauce over the top of the chicken.
2. Cover the cooker and cook on low for 7 to 9 hours, or on high for 3½ to 4 hours.
3. Take the chicken out of the slow cooker. Switch the setting to high, then cover again.
4. Mix the water and cornstarch together until smooth, then stir it into the liquid in the slow cooker. Leave the cover slightly open and cook for 15 to 20 minutes, or until the sauce thickens and bubbles. Serve the sauce over the chicken.

Thai Peanut Wings

Prep time: 20 minutes | Cook time: 3 hours | Serves 8

- 3 pounds (1.4 kg) chicken wing drumettes
- ¼ cup olive oil

Sauce:

- 1 (14-ounce / 397-g) can coconut milk
- ½ cup chicken broth
- 1 cup smooth peanut butter
- ¼ cup firmly packed brown sugar
- 2 tablespoons soy sauce
- 1½ teaspoons salt
- 1 teaspoon sweet paprika
- Freshly ground black pepper
- 2 teaspoons freshly grated ginger
- ¼ teaspoon hot sauce
- ½ cup finely chopped fresh cilantro, for garnish
- ½ cup finely chopped roasted peanuts, for garnish

1. Spray the insert of a 5- to 7-quart slow cooker with nonstick spray. Preheat the broiler for 10 minutes.
2. In a large mixing bowl, combine the wings with olive oil, salt, paprika, and plenty of freshly ground pepper. Toss until the wings are well coated. Arrange them on a wire rack set over a baking sheet and broil for about 5 minutes, until crisp on one side.
3. Flip the wings and broil for another 5 minutes, or until browned and crispy.
4. Take the wings out of the oven. If preparing ahead, let them cool and refrigerate for up to 2 days. Otherwise, transfer directly to the prepared slow-cooker insert.
5. In a small saucepan over medium heat, combine all the sauce ingredients, stirring until blended.
6. Bring the sauce to a boil, then pour it over the wings in the slow cooker, turning them to coat thoroughly.
7. Cover the cooker and cook on high for 3 hours, turning the wings occasionally so they stay coated in sauce.
8. Before serving, garnish the wings with cilantro and peanuts. Keep warm in the cooker until ready to serve.

Chicken with Tropical Barbecue Sauce

Prep time: 5 minutes | Cook time: 3 to 9 hours | Serves 6

- ¼ cup molasses
- 2 tablespoons cider vinegar
- 2 tablespoons Worcestershire sauce
- 2 teaspoons prepared mustard
- ⅛ to ¼ teaspoon hot pepper sauce
- 2 tablespoons orange juice
- 3 whole chicken breasts, halved

1. In a bowl, mix together the molasses, vinegar, Worcestershire sauce, mustard, hot pepper sauce, and orange juice. Brush this mixture over the chicken to coat.
2. Arrange the chicken pieces in the slow cooker.
3. Cover with the lid and cook on low for 7 to 9 hours, or on high for 3 to 4 hours.

Oatmeal Bread and Raisin Stuffed Turkey Tenderloins

Prep time: 15 minutes | Cook time: 7 hours | Serves 2

- 5 slices oatmeal bread, cubed
- 1 small onion, chopped
- 2 garlic cloves, minced
- ½ cup raisins
- 1 egg
- 2 tablespoons butter, melted
- ½ teaspoon salt
- ⅛ teaspoon freshly ground black pepper
- ½ cup chicken stock
- 2 (1 pounds / 454 g) turkey tenderloins
- 2 tablespoons Dijon mustard
- 2 tablespoons honey
- 1 teaspoon poultry seasoning

1. In the slow cooker, combine the bread, onion, garlic, raisins, egg, butter, salt, and pepper, and mix. Drizzle the stock over everything and stir gently to coat.
2. On a platter, rub the turkey tenderloins with the Dijon mustard and honey, and then sprinkle with the poultry seasoning. Place the tenderloins over the bread mixture in the slow cooker.
3. Cover and cook on low for 6 to 7 hours, until the turkey registers 160ºF (71ºC) on a meat thermometer.
4. Slice the turkey and serve it with the stuffing.

Chicken Curry in Cream Sauce

Prep time: 20 minutes | Cook time: 2 to 4 hours | Serves 4 to 6

- 2 (10¾-ounce / 305-g) cans cream of mushroom soup
- 1 soup can water
- 2 teaspoons curry powder
- ⅓ to ½ cup chopped almonds, toasted
- 4 skinless chicken breast halves, cooked and cubed

1. Combine ingredients in slow cooker.
2. Cover and cook on low 2 to 4 hours. Stir occasionally.
3. Serve.

Bistro Chicken Thighs

Prep time: 15 minutes | Cook time: 6 to 8 hours | Serves 6 to 8

- 10 chicken thighs, skin removed
- 1½ teaspoons salt
- ½ teaspoon freshly ground black pepper
- 2 tablespoons extra-virgin olive oil
- 2 tablespoons unsalted butter
- 2 medium onions, coarsely chopped
- 3 cloves garlic, minced
- 2 teaspoons dried thyme
- 1 cup red wine
- 1 (14- to 15-ounce / 397- to 425-g) can crushed tomatoes, with their juice
- ½ cup finely chopped fresh Italian parsley

1. Season the chicken evenly with salt and pepper. Warm the oil in a large skillet over medium heat, then add the chicken and brown it on all sides.
2. Move the browned chicken into the insert of a 5- to 7-quart slow cooker. In the same skillet, melt the butter, then add the onions, garlic, and thyme. Sauté for about 5 minutes, until the onions have softened.
3. Pour in the wine and tomatoes, scraping the browned bits from the bottom of the skillet, and then transfer everything into the slow-cooker insert. Cover and cook on low for 6 to 8 hours, until the chicken is tender and falling from the bone. Skim off any fat that rises to the surface of the sauce.
4. Stir in the parsley just before serving, and keep the dish warm in the cooker.

Tarragon Chicken

Prep time: 25 minutes | Cook time: 3 to 5½ hours | Serves 6

- 2 tablespoons extra-virgin olive oil
- 8 chicken breast halves, skin and bones removed
- Salt and freshly ground black pepper
- 1 clove garlic, minced
- 1 medium onion, finely chopped
- 1 pound (454 g) white button mushrooms, halved or quartered if large
- 1 teaspoon dried tarragon
- ¼ cup dry white wine or vermouth
- 1½ cups chicken broth
- ¼ cup Dijon mustard
- ½ cup heavy cream
- 2 teaspoons cornstarch
- 2 tablespoons finely chopped fresh tarragon, plus additional for garnish

1. In a large skillet over high heat, warm the oil. Season the chicken with 1 teaspoon salt and ½ teaspoon pepper, then add it to the skillet. Brown the chicken on all sides, then move it to the insert of a 5- to 7-quart slow cooker.
2. To the same skillet, add the garlic, onion, mushrooms, and dried tarragon. Sauté for 7 to 10 minutes, until the onion softens and the mushrooms release their liquid, which should then evaporate. Pour in the wine to deglaze, scraping up the browned bits from the pan.
3. Pour everything from the skillet into the slow-cooker insert. Stir in the broth and mustard, then cover and cook on high for 2½ hours or on low for 4 to 5 hours.
4. Mix the cream, cornstarch, and two tablespoons of fresh tarragon into the cooker. Cover again and cook for 15 minutes on high or 30 minutes on low, until the sauce thickens. Adjust seasoning with salt and pepper.
5. Serve the chicken hot, topped with extra fresh tarragon as garnish.

One-Pot Chicken Supper

Prep time: 5 minutes | Cook time: 6 to 8 hours | Serves 4

- 4 boneless, skinless chicken breast halves
- 1 (10¾-ounce / 305-g) can cream of chicken or celery or mushroom soup
- ⅓ cup milk
- 1 package Stove Top stuffing mix and seasoning packet
- 1⅔ cups water

1. Place chicken in slow cooker.
2. Combine soup and milk. Pour over chicken.
3. Combine stuffing mix, seasoning packet, and water. Spoon over chicken.
4. Cover. Cook on low 6 to 8 hours.

Pumpkin Black Bean Turkey Chili

Prep time: 20 minutes | Cook time: 7 to 8 hours | Serves 10 to 12

- 1 cup chopped onions
- 1 cup chopped yellow bell pepper
- 3 garlic cloves, minced
- 2 tablespoons oil
- 1½ teaspoons dried oregano
- 1½ to 2 teaspoons ground cumin
- 2 teaspoons chili powder
- 2 (15-ounce / 425-g) cans black beans, rinsed and drained
- 2½ cups cooked turkey, chopped
- 1 (16-ounce / 454-g) can pumpkin
- 1 (14½-ounce / 411-g) can diced tomatoes
- 3 cups chicken broth

1. Heat the oil in a skillet and sauté the onions, yellow pepper, and garlic for about 8 minutes, or until softened.
2. Add the oregano, cumin, and chili powder, stirring them into the vegetables.
3. Cook for 1 more minute, then transfer everything to the slow cooker. Add the rest of the ingredients and stir to combine.
4. Cover with the lid and cook on low for 7 to 8 hours.

Poached Chicken Breasts

Prep time: 15 minutes | Cook time: 4 to 5 hours | Serves 8

- 2 cups chicken broth
- 3 whole black peppercorns
- ½ teaspoon dried thyme
- 12 chicken breast halves, skin and bones removed

1. Mix together the broth, peppercorns, and thyme in the insert of a 5- to 7-quart slow cooker. Place the chicken breasts in the slow cooker, stacking them in an even layer.
2. Cover and cook on low for 4 to 5 hours, until the chicken is cooked through and tender. Let the chicken cool and remove it from the slow cooker. Refrigerate for 2 days or freeze for up to 10 weeks.

Chicken with Mushrooms and Shallots

Prep time: 15 minutes | Cook time: 6 to 8 hours | Serves 2

- 1 teaspoon unsalted butter, at room temperature, or extra-virgin olive oil
- 2 cups thinly sliced cremini mushrooms
- 1 teaspoon fresh thyme
- 2 garlic cloves, minced
- 1 shallot, minced
- 3 tablespoons dry sherry
- 2 bone-in, skinless chicken thighs, about 6 ounces (170 g) each
- ⅛ teaspoon sea salt
- Freshly ground black pepper

1. Use the butter to grease the inside of the slow cooker.
2. Add the mushrooms, thyme, garlic, and shallot to the cooker, tossing lightly to mix, then pour in the sherry.
3. Season the chicken thighs with salt and pepper, then place them over the mushroom mixture.
4. Cover with the lid and cook on low for 6 to 8 hours.

Turkey in Tomato Braise

Prep time: 20 minutes | Cook time: 3 hours | Serves 8

- 6 strips thick-cut bacon, cut into ½-inch pieces
- 1 medium onion, finely chopped
- 1 teaspoon dried basil
- 1 pound (454 g) cremini mushrooms, quartered
- 1½ teaspoons salt
- ½ teaspoon freshly ground black pepper
- 1 (28- to 32-ounce / 794- to 907-g) can crushed tomatoes
- ½ cup finely chopped fresh Italian parsley
- 4 turkey thighs, skin removed

1. Cook the bacon in a sauté pan over medium heat until it renders some fat and is beginning to turn crisp. Add the onion and basil and sauté until the onion is softened, about 3 minutes.
2. Add the mushrooms, salt, and pepper and sauté until the mushrooms begin to colour, 7 to 10 minutes. Transfer the mixture to the insert of a 5- to 7-quart slow cooker. Add the tomatoes and parsley and stir to combine. Add the thighs in the sauce.
3. Cover and cook on high for 3 hours, until the thighs are cooked through and register 175ºF (79ºC) on an instant-read thermometer. Skim off any fat from the top of the sauce. Remove the thighs from the sauce and discard the bones.
4. Cut the meat into serving-sized pieces and return to the sauce.
5. Serve from the cooker set on warm.

Tender Turkey Breast

Prep time: 5 minutes | Cook time: 2 to 9 hours | Serves 10

- 1 (6-pound / 2.7-kg) boneless or bone-in turkey breast
- 2 to 3 tablespoons water

1. Put the turkey breast into the slow cooker and pour in the water.
2. Cover with the lid and cook on high for 2 to 4 hours, or on low for 4 to 9 hours, until the meat is tender but not dry or mushy.
3. Turn the turkey breast once during the cooking process.
4. For a browned finish, transfer the cooked turkey to the oven and bake uncovered at 325ºF (165ºC) for 15 to 20 minutes.

Green Chili Chicken Stew

Prep time: 20 minutes | Cook time: 8 hours | Serves 6

- 1½ pounds (680 g) boneless, skinless chicken thighs
- 2 pounds (907 g) tomatillos, husked, cleaned, and puréed
- 1 medium onion, finely chopped
- 3 garlic cloves, minced
- ½ cup finely chopped fresh cilantro
- 2½ cups low-sodium chicken stock
- 1 tablespoon chili powder, preferably ancho
- 1 teaspoon ground cumin
- 1 teaspoon kosher salt, plus more for seasoning
- 1 (14½-ounce / 411-g) can cannellini or pinto beans, drained and rinsed
- Freshly ground black pepper
- 1 cup crushed tortilla chips, for garnish
- ½ cup sour cream, for garnish
- 1 medium red onion, finely chopped, for garnish
- 1 lime, cut into wedges, for garnish

1. Put the chicken in the slow cooker, along with the puréed tomatillos, onion, garlic, cilantro, chicken stock, chili powder, cumin, salt, and beans. Stir to combine. Cover and cook on low for 8 hours.
2. Use two forks to shred the chicken. Season with additional salt and pepper, as needed. Ladle into the bowls and garnish with the tortilla chips, sour cream, red onion, and a squirt of lime.

Chicken Azteca

Prep time: 20 minutes | Cook time: 2½ to 6½ hours | Serves 10 to 12

- 2 (15-ounce / 425-g) cans black beans, drained
- 4 cups frozen corn kernels
- 2 garlic cloves, minced
- ¾ teaspoon ground cumin
- 2 cups chunky salsa, divided
- 10 skinless, boneless chicken breast halves
- 2 (8-ounce / 227-g) packages cream cheese, cubed
- Rice, cooked
- Shredded Cheddar cheese

1. Place the beans, corn, garlic, cumin, and half of the salsa into the slow cooker and stir to combine.
2. Lay the chicken breasts on top, then pour the remaining salsa over them.
3. Cover and cook on high for 2 to 3 hours, or on low for 4 to 6 hours.
4. Remove the chicken, cut it into bite-sized pieces, and return it to the cooker.
5. Add the cream cheese and cook on high until it has melted into the sauce.
6. Serve the chicken mixture over cooked rice and sprinkle with shredded cheese before serving.

Chicken in Coconut Curry

Prep time: 15 minutes | Cook time: 3 to 4 hours | Serves 6

- 1 tablespoon coconut oil
- 1 teaspoon cumin seeds
- 2 medium onions, grated
- 7 to 8 ounces (198 to 227 g) canned plum tomatoes
- 1 teaspoon salt
- 1 teaspoon turmeric
- ½ to 1 teaspoon Kashmiri chili powder (optional)
- 2 to 3 fresh green chiles, chopped
- 1 cup coconut cream
- 12 chicken thighs, skinned, trimmed, and cut into bite-size chunks
- 1 teaspoon garam masala
- Handful fresh coriander leaves, chopped

1. Heat the oil in a frying pan (or in the slow cooker if you have a sear setting). Add the cumin seeds. When sizzling and aromatic, add the onions and cook until they are browning, about 5 to 7 minutes.
2. In a blender, purée the tomatoes and add them to the pan with the salt, turmeric, chili powder (if using), and fresh green chiles.
3. Stir together and put everything in the slow cooker. Pour in the coconut cream. Add the meat and stir to coat with the sauce.
4. Cover and cook on low for 4 hours, or on high for 3 hours.
5. Taste the sauce and adjust the seasoning. If the sauce is very liquidy, turn the cooker to high and cook for 30 minutes more with the lid off.
6. Add the garam masala and throw in the fresh coriander leaves to serve.

Chicken and Vegetable Medley

Prep time: 15 minutes | Cook time: 6 to 8 hours | Serves 4

- 4 bone-in chicken breast halves
- 1 small head of cabbage, quartered
- 1 (1-pound / 454-g) package baby carrots
- 2 (14½-ounce / 411-g) cans Mexican-flavoured stewed tomatoes

1. Place all ingredients in slow cooker in order listed.
2. Cover and cook on low 6 to 8 hours, or until chicken and vegetables are tender.

Spicy Asian Braised Napa Cabbage Wraps

Prep time: 25 minutes | Cook time: 1½ to 2 hours | Serves 8

- 1 head Napa cabbage
- 2 cups chicken broth
- ½ cup soy sauce
- 4 slices fresh ginger
- 2 tablespoons vegetable oil
- 2 cloves garlic, minced
- 1 teaspoon freshly grated ginger
- 6 canned water chestnuts, finely chopped
- 2 chicken breast halves, skin and bones removed, finely chopped
- 4 green onions, finely chopped, using the white and tender green parts
- 2 tablespoons hoisin sauce
- 1 tablespoon cornstarch mixed with 2 tablespoons water

1. Core the cabbage carefully, then separate the leaves without tearing them. In a large stockpot, combine the broth, soy sauce, and ginger, and bring the mixture to a boil.
2. Working one at a time, blanch the cabbage leaves for about 30 seconds until pliable. Drain well and set aside. Pour the hot broth mixture into the insert of a 5- to 7-quart slow cooker, cover it, and keep on warm as you prepare the filling.
3. Place a sauté pan over high heat and warm the oil. Add the garlic, ginger, and water chestnuts; cook for 30 seconds, stirring constantly. Add the chicken and continue cooking for 3 to 5 minutes, until the meat turns white.
4. Move the mixture into a bowl, then stir in the green onions and hoisin sauce. Put 2 to 3 tablespoons of filling at the base of each cabbage leaf, fold in the sides, and roll tightly. Arrange the rolls neatly on a rack inside the slow cooker.
5. Cover and cook on high for 1½ to 2 hours, until the chicken is done. Remove the rolls and set aside. Strain the broth through a fine-mesh sieve into a saucepan, bring it to a boil, stir in the cornstarch mixture, and let it boil again until thickened.
6. Serve the cabbage rolls with the prepared sauce on the side.

Chapter 5

Beef, Pork, and Lamb

Chapter 5 Beef, Pork, and Lamb

Baked Beans with Pork Chops

Prep time: 10 minutes | Cook time: 4 to 6 hours | Serves 6

- 2 (16½-ounce / 468-g) cans baked beans
- 6 rib pork chops, ½-inch thick
- 1½ teaspoons prepared mustard
- 1½ tablespoons brown sugar
- 1½ tablespoons ketchup
- 6 onion slices

1. Pour baked beans into bottom of greased slow cooker.
2. Layer pork chops over beans.
3. Spread mustard over pork chops. Sprinkle with brown sugar and drizzle with ketchup.
4. Top with onion slices.
5. Cover. Cook on high 4 to 6 hours.

Beef Burgundy Stew

Prep time: 30 minutes | Cook time: 6¼ to 8¼ hours | Serves 8

- 2 slices lean turkey bacon, cut in squares
- 2 pounds (907 g) lean sirloin tip or round steak, cubed
- ¼ cup flour
- 1 teaspoon salt
- ½ teaspoon seasoned salt
- ¼ teaspoon dried marjoram
- ½ teaspoon dried thyme
- ¼ teaspoon black pepper
- 1 garlic clove, minced
- 1 low-sodium beef bouillon cube, crushed
- 1 cup burgundy wine
- ¼ pound (113 g) fresh mushrooms, sliced
- 2 tablespoons cornstarch
- 2 tablespoons cold water

1. Cook bacon in nonstick skillet until browned. Remove bacon, reserving drippings.
2. Coat beef with flour and brown on all sides in bacon drippings.
3. Combine steak, bacon drippings, bacon, seasonings, garlic, bouillon, and wine in slow cooker.
4. Cover. Cook on low 6 to 8 hours.
5. Add mushrooms.
6. Dissolve cornstarch in water. Add to slow cooker.
7. Cover. Cook on high 15 minutes.
8. Serve.

Italian Roast with Potatoes

Prep time: 30 minutes | Cook time: 6 to 7 hours | Serves 8

- 6 medium potatoes, peeled if you wish, and quartered
- 1 large onion, sliced
- 1 (3- to 4-pound / 1.4- to 1.8-kg) boneless beef roast
- 1 (26-ounce / 737-g) jar tomato and basil pasta sauce, divided
- ½ cup water
- 3 beef bouillon cubes

1. Arrange the potatoes and onion in the bottom of the slow cooker.
2. While that sits, brown the roast on both sides in a nonstick skillet.
3. Set the browned roast over the vegetables in the cooker and pour any skillet drippings on top of the meat.
4. In a small bowl, combine 1 cup pasta sauce with ½ cup water and stir in the bouillon cubes. Spoon this mixture over the beef.
5. Cover the slow cooker and cook on low for 6 to 7 hours, until the meat is tender but not dried out.
6. Move the roast and vegetables to a serving platter and cover with foil to keep warm.
7. Measure 1 cup of the cooking juices from the slow cooker, pour into a medium saucepan, and stir in the remaining pasta sauce. Heat until warmed through.
8. Slice or cube the beef and serve with the heated sauce spooned over the top.

Chili Hot Dogs

Prep time: 10 minutes | Cook time: 2 to 3 hours | Serves 4 to 5

- 1 package hot dogs, cut into ¾-inch slices
- 1 (28-ounce / 794-g) can baked beans
- 1 teaspoon prepared mustard
- 1 teaspoon instant minced onion
- ⅓ cup chili sauce

1. Place all the ingredients into the slow cooker and stir to combine.
2. Cover with the lid and cook on low for 2 to 3 hours.
3. Serve directly from the cooker.

Classic Meat Loaf

Prep time: 15 minutes | Cook time: 2 to 8 hours | Serves 8

- ½ cup ketchup, divided
- 2 pounds (907 g) ground beef
- 2 eggs
- ⅔ cup dry quick oats
- 1 envelope dry onion soup mix

1. Reserve 2 tablespoons ketchup. Combine ground beef, eggs, dry oats, soup mix, and remaining ketchup. Shape into loaf. Place in slow cooker.
2. Top with remaining ketchup.
3. Cover and cook on low for 6 to 8 hours, or on high for 2 to 4 hours.

Bean Tator Tot Casserole

Prep time: 10 minutes | Cook time: 4 hours | Serves 6

- 1 pound (454 g) ground beef
- ½ teaspoon salt
- ¼ teaspoon pepper
- 1 onion, chopped
- 1 (1-pound / 454-g) bag frozen string beans
- 1 (10¾-ounce / 305-g) can cream of mushroom soup
- 1 cup shredded cheese
- 1 (21-ounce / 595-g) bag frozen tater tots

1. Place the raw ground beef in the bottom of the slow cooker, crumbling it evenly, then season with salt and pepper.
2. Layer the rest of the ingredients on top of the beef in the order given.
3. Cover and cook on high for 1 hour, then lower the heat to low and continue cooking for 3 more hours.

Beef Tongue

Prep time: 20 minutes | Cook time: 7 to 8 hours | Serves 6

- 1 beef tongue, fresh or smoked
- 2 scant tablespoons salt
- 1½ cups water
- 1 bay leaf
- 2 lemons, squeezed, or 2 onions quartered
- 6 peppercorns

1. Place the washed tongue directly into the slow cooker.
2. Mix the remaining ingredients together in a bowl, then pour the mixture evenly over the tongue.
3. Cover the cooker and cook on low for 7 to 8 hours, or until the meat is fork-tender. Once slightly cooled, carefully pull off the outer skin.
4. Cut the meat into slices and serve while hot.

Hearty Meatball Stew

Prep time: 25 minutes | Cook time: 4 to 5 hours | Serves 8

- 2 pounds (907 g) ground beef
- ½ teaspoon salt
- ½ teaspoon pepper
- 6 medium potatoes, cubed
- 1 large onion, sliced
- 6 medium carrots, sliced
- 1 cup ketchup
- 1 cup water
- 1½ teaspoons balsamic vinegar
- 1 teaspoon dried basil
- 1 teaspoon dried oregano
- ½ teaspoon salt
- ½ teaspoon pepper

1. Combine beef, ½ teaspoon salt, and ½ teaspoon pepper. Mix well. Shape into 1-inch balls. Brown meatballs in saucepan over medium heat. Drain.
2. Place potatoes, onion, and carrots in slow cooker. Top with meatballs.
3. Combine ketchup, water, vinegar, basil, oregano, ½ teaspoon salt, and ½ teaspoon pepper. Pour over meatballs.
4. Cover. Cook on high 4 to 5 hours, or until vegetables are tender.

Cola-Marinated Barbecue Steak

Prep time: 15 minutes | Cook time: 5½ to 6½ hours | Serves 24

- 1 (4-pound / 1.8-kg) round steak, ¾-inch thick, cut into (3-inch) cubes
- 2 cups ketchup
- 1 cup cola
- ½ cup chopped onion
- 2 garlic cloves, minced
- Nonstick cooking spray

1. Spray slow cooker with nonstick cooking spray.
2. Place beef pieces in cooker.
3. Mix remaining ingredients in a large bowl and pour over meat.
4. Cover and cook on high 5 to 6 hours.
5. About 30 minutes before serving, remove beef from slow cooker and shred with 2 forks. Return beef to slow cooker and mix well with sauce.
6. Cover and cook on high an additional 20 minutes.
7. Serve.

Fiery Curry Beef

Prep time: 10 minutes | Cook time: 7 to 8 hours | Serves 6

- 1 tablespoon extra-virgin olive oil
- 1 pound (454 g) beef chuck roast, cut into 2-inch pieces
- 1 sweet onion, chopped
- 1 red bell pepper, diced
- 2 cups coconut milk
- 2 tablespoons hot curry powder
- 1 tablespoon coconut aminos
- 2 teaspoons grated fresh ginger
- 2 teaspoons minced garlic
- 1 cup shredded baby bok choy

1. Grease the slow-cooker insert lightly with olive oil.
2. Place the beef, onion, and bell pepper into the insert.
3. In a medium bowl, whisk the coconut milk with the curry, coconut aminos, ginger, and garlic. Pour this mixture over the beef and vegetables, stirring to blend.
4. Cover and cook on low for 7 to 8 hours.
5. Add the bok choy, stir gently, and let it stand for 15 minutes.
6. Serve hot.

Indian Meatballs with Mint

Prep time: 20 minutes | Cook time: 2 to 4 hours | Serves 6 to 8

- 1¾ pounds (794 g) lean ground lamb
- 2 teaspoons ground cumin
- 2 teaspoons chili powder, divided
- 3 teaspoons garam masala
- Handful fresh mint, chopped
- ½ teaspoon ground cinnamon
- 2 teaspoons salt, divided
- 2 large onions
- 6 garlic cloves
- 2-inch piece fresh ginger
- 2 to 3 fresh green chiles
- 1 (14-ounce / 397-g) can plum tomatoes
- 1 tablespoon rapeseed oil
- 1 teaspoon turmeric
- 1 teaspoon dried fenugreek leaves
- 1 to 1¼ cups hot water
- Handful fresh coriander leaves, finely chopped

1. In a large mixing bowl, add the lamb, cumin, 1 teaspoon chili powder, garam masala, mint, cinnamon, and 1 teaspoon of salt. Mix well using your hands to ensure the spices are evenly distributed.
2. Rub a little oil on your hands to prevent the meat from sticking to them. Then take a small amount of the meat and roll it in your palms to make a meatball. Make sure it is smooth all over. Set aside and repeat with the remaining mixture. You should get about 24 kofta.
3. In a blender, mince the onions, garlic, ginger, and chiles—not to a purée, just so everything is chopped—and set aside. Blend the tomatoes to a purée.
4. Heat the slow cooker to high and add the oil. Carefully fry the kofta in batches so they brown all over. Remove the kofta and set them on some paper towels to drain.
5. Add the onion mixture to the cooker and cook for 5 to 6 minutes in the remaining oil. Add the tomatoes, turmeric, dried fenugreek leaves, the remaining 1 teaspoon of chili powder, and remaining 1 teaspoon of salt. Stir together, add the kofta to the cooker, and toss to coat with the sauce for a few minutes.
6. If you like a gravy, add enough hot water so the kofta are half covered. If you prefer a thicker sauce, use less water.
7. Cover and cook for 4 hours on low, or for 2 to 3 hours on high. If you want to leave it to cook for longer, that's fine, too.
8. Throw in the garam masala and coriander leaves just before serving.

Easy Beef Tortillas

Prep time: 20 minutes | Cook time: 1½ to 3 hours | Serves 6

- 1½ pounds (680 g) ground beef
- 1 (10¾-ounce / 305-g) can cream of chicken soup
- 2½ cups crushed tortilla chips, divided
- 1 (16-ounce / 454-g) jar salsa
- 1½ cups shredded Cheddar cheese
- Nonstick cooking spray

1. In a nonstick skillet, brown the ground beef, then drain off any fat. Stir in the soup until combined.
2. Coat the inside of the slow cooker with nonstick spray. Spread 1½ cups of tortilla chips in the bottom, then layer with the beef mixture, followed by the salsa, and finally the cheese.
3. Cover and cook on high for 1½ hours, or set to low and cook for 3 hours.
4. Just before serving, sprinkle the top with the remaining chips.

Rich Low-Fat Slow-Cooker Beef Barbecue

Prep time: 20 minutes | Cook time: 4 hours | Serves 12

- 1 pound (454 g) extra-lean ground beef
- 2 cups celery, chopped fine
- 1 cup onions, chopped
- 1 tablespoon whipped butter
- 2 tablespoons red wine vinegar
- 1 tablespoon brown sugar
- 3 tablespoons Worcestershire sauce
- 1 teaspoon salt
- 1 teaspoon yellow prepared mustard
- 1 cup ketchup
- 2 cups water

1. Brown ground beef, celery, and onions in a nonstick skillet.
2. Combine all ingredients in slow cooker.
3. Cover and cook on high for 4 hours.
4. Serve.

Pork with Lemon

Prep time: 15 minutes | Cook time: 7 to 8 hours | Serves 6

- 3 tablespoons extra-virgin olive oil, divided
- 1 tablespoon butter
- 2 pounds (907 g) pork loin roast
- ½ teaspoon salt
- ¼ teaspoon freshly ground black pepper
- ¼ cup chicken broth
- Juice and zest of 1 lemon
- 1 tablespoon minced garlic
- ½ cup heavy (whipping) cream

1. Lightly grease the insert of the slow cooker with 1 tablespoon of the olive oil.
2. In a large skillet over medium-high heat, heat the remaining 2 tablespoons of the olive oil and the butter.
3. Lightly season the pork with salt and pepper. Add the pork to the skillet and brown the roast on all sides for about 10 minutes. Transfer it to the insert.
4. In a small bowl, stir together the broth, lemon juice and zest, and garlic.
5. Add the broth mixture to the roast.
6. Cover, and cook on low for 7 to 8 hours.
7. Stir in the heavy cream and serve.

Pork Roast with Cranberries

Prep time: 15 minutes | Cook time: 7 to 8 hours | Serves 6

- 3 tablespoons extra-virgin olive oil, divided
- 2 tablespoons butter
- 2 pounds (907 g) pork shoulder roast
- 1 teaspoon ground cinnamon
- ¼ teaspoon allspice
- ¼ teaspoon salt
- ⅛ teaspoon freshly ground black pepper
- ½ cup cranberries
- ½ cup chicken broth
- ½ cup granulated erythritol
- 2 tablespoons Dijon mustard
- Juice and zest of ½ orange
- 1 scallion, white and green parts, chopped, for garnish

1. Lightly grease the insert of the slow cooker with 1 tablespoon of the olive oil.
2. In a large skillet over medium-high heat, heat the remaining 2 tablespoons of the olive oil and the butter.
3. Lightly season the pork with cinnamon, allspice, salt, and pepper. Add the pork to the skillet and brown on all sides for about 10 minutes. Transfer to the insert.
4. In a small bowl, stir together the cranberries, broth, erythritol, mustard, and orange juice and zest, and add the mixture to the pork.
5. Cover and cook on low for 7 to 8 hours.
6. Serve topped with the scallion.

Corned Beef and Cabbage with Fruit

Prep time: 10 minutes | Cook time: 5 to 12 hours | Serves 6

- 2 medium onions, sliced
- 1 (2½- to 3-pound / 1.1- to 1.4-kg) corned beef brisket
- 1 cup apple juice
- ¼ cup brown sugar, packed
- 2 teaspoons finely shredded orange peel
- 6 whole cloves
- 2 teaspoons prepared mustard
- 6 cabbage wedges

1. Place onions in slow cooker. Place beef on top of onions.
2. Combine apple juice, brown sugar, orange peel, cloves, and mustard. Pour over meat.
3. Place cabbage on top.
4. Cover. Cook on low 10 to 12 hours, or on high 5 to 6 hours.

Chili con Carne

Prep time: 15 minutes | Cook time: 5 to 6 hours | Serves 8

- 1 pound (454 g) ground beef
- 1 cup chopped onions
- ¾ cup chopped green peppers
- 1 garlic clove, minced
- 1 (14½-ounce / 411-g) can tomatoes, cut up
- 1 (16-ounce / 454-g) can kidney beans, drained
- 1 (8-ounce / 227-g) can tomato sauce
- 2 teaspoons chili powder
- ½ teaspoon dried basil

1. In a saucepan, brown the beef together with the onion, green pepper, and garlic, then drain off the excess fat.
2. Transfer everything to the slow cooker and add the remaining ingredients, stirring to combine.
3. Cover with the lid and cook on low for 5 to 6 hours.
4. Serve hot.

Cinco de Mayo Pork

Prep time: 15 minutes | Cook time: 4 to 8 hours | Serves 6 to 8

- 2 tablespoons vegetable oil
- 1 teaspoon ground cumin
- ½ teaspoon chili powder
- 2 cloves garlic, minced
- 3 pounds (1.4 kg) boneless pork shoulder meat, excess fat removed, cut into 2-inch pieces
- 2 teaspoons salt
- 1 cup prepared salsa (medium, or hot if you like a bit more heat)
- ½ cup beef broth
- 1 (16-ounce / 454-g) package frozen corn, defrosted
- Flour or corn tortillas for serving

1. Warm the oil in a large skillet over medium heat. Add the cumin, chili powder, and garlic, sautéing for about 1 minute until the spices and garlic become fragrant.
2. Season the pork with salt, then brown it on all sides in the skillet with the spices. Move the pork to the insert of a 5- to 7-quart slow cooker. Pour the salsa and broth into the skillet, scraping up any browned bits from the bottom.
3. Transfer everything from the skillet into the slow-cooker insert and stir in the corn. Cover and cook on high for 4 hours or on low for 8 hours, until the pork is tender. Serve with warm tortillas.

Festive Cocktail Meatballs

Prep time: 35 minutes | Cook time: 4 hours | Serves 6

- 2 pounds (907 g) ground beef
- ⅓ cup ketchup
- 3 teaspoons dry bread crumbs
- 1 egg, beaten
- 2 teaspoons onion flakes
- ¾ teaspoon garlic salt
- ½ teaspoon pepper
- 1 cup ketchup
- 1 cup packed brown sugar
- 1 (6-ounce / 170-g) can tomato paste
- ¼ cup soy sauce
- ¼ cup cider vinegar
- 1 to 1½ teaspoons hot pepper sauce

1. In a bowl, mix together the ground beef, ⅓ cup ketchup, bread crumbs, egg, onion flakes, garlic salt, and pepper until well combined. Shape into 1-inch meatballs, place them on a jelly roll pan, and bake at 350°F (180°C) for about 18 minutes, or until browned. Transfer the meatballs to the slow cooker.
2. In another bowl, combine 1 cup ketchup with the brown sugar, tomato paste, soy sauce, vinegar, and hot pepper sauce. Pour this sauce over the meatballs.
3. Cover with the lid and cook on low for 4 hours.

Ranch-Style Beef

Prep time: 10 minutes | Cook time: 4 to 9 hours | Serves 10 to 12

- 1 (3- to 3½-pound / 1.4- to 1.6-kg) boneless beef chuck roast
- 1 cup thinly sliced onions
- 1 (10¾-ounce / 305-g) can cream of celery soup
- 1 (4-ounce / 113-g) can sliced mushrooms
- 1 (12-ounce / 340-g) can beer
- ½ cup ketchup
- 1 large bay leaf
- ½ teaspoon salt
- ¼ teaspoon lemon pepper
- 2 tablespoons chopped fresh parsley, or 1½ teaspoons dried parsley

1. Place roast in slow cooker.
2. Combine remaining ingredients. Pour over roast.
3. Cover. Cook on low 7 to 9 hours or on Medium setting 4 to 6 hours, until meat is tender.
4. Remove bay leaf.
5. Shred roast with two forks. Mix meat through sauce.
6. Serve.

Pot Roast Italiano

Prep time: 20 minutes | Cook time: 4 to 10 hours | Serves 6 to 8

- 1 tablespoon extra-virgin olive oil
- 1 bottom round roast (about 3 to 3½ pounds / 1.4 to 1.6 kg), tied with butcher's twine
- 3 cloves garlic, minced
- Salt and freshly ground black pepper
- 2 large sweet onions, such as Vidalia, coarsely chopped
- 1 tablespoon dried rosemary, crumbled
- 1 cup Zinfandel wine
- 4 dried porcini mushrooms, crumbled
- 1 (15-ounce / 425-g) can chopped tomatoes, with their juice
- 2 tablespoons all-purpose flour
- 2 tablespoons unsalted butter
- ¼ cup finely chopped fresh Italian parsley for garnish

1. In a large skillet over high heat, warm the oil. Rub the meat with garlic, 1½ teaspoons salt, and 1 teaspoon pepper, then place it in the skillet and brown thoroughly on all sides.
2. Move the browned meat into the insert of a 5- to 7-quart slow cooker. Using the same skillet, sauté the onions and rosemary for about 3 minutes, until fragrant and slightly softened, then transfer them to the slow cooker.
3. Stir in the wine, dried mushrooms, and tomatoes. Cover and cook on high for 4 to 5 hours or on low for 10 hours, until the meat is fork-tender.
4. Take the meat out of the slow cooker, cover it with foil, and let it rest for 15 minutes.
5. Pour the cooking liquid into a saucepan and bring it to a boil. Let it boil for about 10 minutes to intensify the flavour. Mix the flour and butter together in a small bowl to form a paste, then whisk it into the sauce gradually until thickened.
6. Remove the saucepan from the heat and stir in the parsley. Adjust with more salt and pepper if needed. Slice the meat, spoon some sauce over the top, and serve, with the remaining sauce passed at the table.

Herb-Braised Pork Chops

Prep time: 15 minutes | Cook time: 7 to 8 hours | Serves 6

- ¼ cup extra-virgin olive oil, divided
- 1½ pounds (680 g) pork loin chops
- Salt, for seasoning
- Freshly ground black pepper, for seasoning
- 1 cup chicken broth
- ½ sweet onion, chopped
- 2 teaspoons minced garlic
- 1 teaspoon dried thyme
- 1 teaspoon dried oregano
- 1 cup heavy (whipping) cream
- 1 tablespoon chopped fresh basil, for garnish

1. Grease the slow-cooker insert with 1 tablespoon of olive oil.
2. Warm the remaining 3 tablespoons of olive oil in a large skillet over medium-high heat.
3. Season the pork chops lightly with salt and pepper, then brown them in the skillet for about 5 minutes. Transfer the browned chops to the slow-cooker insert.
4. In a medium bowl, mix together the broth, onion, garlic, thyme, and oregano.
5. Pour the broth mixture over the pork chops in the insert.
6. Cover with the lid and cook on low for 7 to 8 hours.
7. Stir in the heavy cream just before serving.
8. Garnish with fresh basil and serve.

Bandito Chili Dogs

Prep time: 10 minutes | Cook time: 3 to 3½ hours | Serves 10

- 1 pound (454 g) hot dogs
- 2 (15-ounce / 425-g) cans chili, with or without beans
- 1 (10¾-ounce / 305-g) can condensed Cheddar cheese soup
- 1 (4-ounce / 113-g) can chopped green chilies
- 10 hot dog buns
- 1 medium onion, chopped
- 1 to 2 cups corn chips, coarsely crushed
- 1 cup shredded Cheddar cheese

1. Put the hot dogs into the slow cooker.
2. Mix the chili, soup, and green chilies in a bowl, then pour the mixture over the hot dogs.
3. Cover with the lid and cook on low for 3 to 3½ hours.
4. Serve the hot dogs in buns, topping each with the chili mixture, onion, corn chips, and cheese.

Meatballs with Beef and Ham

Prep time: 20 minutes | Cook time: 2¾ to 3¾ hours | Serves 5 to 7

- 1½ pounds (680 g) ground beef
- 1 (4½-ounce / 128-g) can deviled ham
- ⅔ cup evaporated milk
- 2 eggs, beaten slightly
- 1 tablespoon grated onion
- 2 cups soft bread crumbs
- 1 teaspoon salt
- ¼ teaspoon allspice
- ¼ teaspoon pepper
- ¼ cup flour
- ¼ cup water
- 1 tablespoon ketchup
- 2 teaspoons dill weed
- 1 cup sour cream

1. Combine beef, ham, milk, eggs, onion, bread crumbs, salt, allspice, and pepper. Shape into 2-inch meatballs. Arrange in slow cooker.
2. Cover. Cook on low 2½ to 3½ hours. Turn control to high.
3. Dissolve flour in water until smooth. Stir in ketchup and dill weed. Add to meatballs, stirring gently.
4. Cook on high 15 to 20 minutes, or until slightly thickened.
5. Turn off heat. Stir in sour cream.
6. Serve.

Baked Tortilla Casserole

Prep time: 20 minutes | Cook time: 3¼ to 4¼ hours | Serves 4

- 4 to 6 white or whole wheat tortillas, divided
- 1 pound (454 g) ground beef
- 1 envelope dry taco seasoning
- 1 (16-ounce / 454-g) can fat-free refried beans
- 1½ cups shredded low-fat cheese of your choice, divided
- 3 to 4 tablespoons sour cream (optional)
- Nonstick cooking spray

1. Spray the inside of the cooker with nonstick cooking spray. Tear about ¾ of the tortillas into pieces and line the sides and bottom of the slow cooker.
2. Brown the ground beef in a nonstick skillet. Drain. Return to skillet and mix in taco seasoning.
3. Layer refried beans, browned and seasoned meat, 1 cup cheese, and sour cream if you wish, over tortilla pieces.
4. Place remaining tortilla pieces on top.
5. Sprinkle with remaining cheese. Cover and cook on low 3 to 4 hours.

Sirloin steak

Prep time: 20 minutes | Cook time: 4 to 9 hours | Serves 6 to 8

- 1 (2½- to 3-pound / 1.1- to 1.4-kg) sirloin roast
- Salt and freshly ground black pepper
- 3 tablespoons olive oil
- 2 large sweet onions, such as Vidalia, coarsely chopped
- 2 teaspoons dried thyme
- 3 cups beef broth
- 2 tablespoons Worcestershire sauce
- 24 golf ball–sized Yukon gold or red potatoes
- 2 tablespoons unsalted butter
- 2 tablespoons all-purpose flour

1. Rub the roast evenly with 1½ teaspoons salt and 1 teaspoon pepper. In a large skillet over high heat, heat the oil and sear the meat on all sides until nicely browned.
2. Place the roast into the insert of a 5- to 7-quart slow cooker. Add the onions and thyme to the same skillet and sauté for 3 to 4 minutes, just until the onions soften. Transfer this mixture into the slow cooker, then pour in the broth and Worcestershire, arranging the potatoes around the roast.
3. Cover with the lid and cook for 4 to 5 hours on high or 8 to 9 hours on low. When done, remove the roast and potatoes, cover loosely with foil, and let rest for about 15 minutes.
4. Skim the fat from the top of the sauce. If you like, strain the liquid through a fine-mesh sieve into a saucepan. In a small bowl, mix together the butter and flour to form a paste.
5. Bring the sauce to a boil, whisking in the butter mixture gradually, allowing it to return to a boil after each addition. Taste and season with salt and pepper as needed.
6. Slice the roast, spoon some of the sauce over the meat, and serve. Offer any extra sauce at the table.

Chapter 6

Fish and Seafood

Chapter 6 Fish and Seafood

Smoked Salmon and Potato Casserole

Prep time: 10 minutes | Cook time: 8 hours | Serves 2

- 1 teaspoon butter, at room temperature, or extra-virgin olive oil
- 2 eggs
- 1 cup 2% milk
- 1 teaspoon dried dill
- ⅛ teaspoon sea salt
- Freshly ground black pepper
- 2 medium russet potatoes, peeled and sliced thin
- 4 ounces (113 g) smoked salmon

1. Use the butter to grease the inside of the slow cooker.
2. In a small bowl, whisk the eggs, milk, dill, salt, and a few twists of black pepper until well combined.
3. Arrange one-third of the potatoes in an even layer on the bottom of the slow cooker, then add one-third of the salmon. Pour over one-third of the egg mixture. Repeat the layering process with the rest of the potatoes, salmon, and egg mixture.
4. Cover with the lid and cook on low for 8 hours or overnight.

Spicy Tomato Basil Mussels

Prep time: 15 minutes | Cook time: 7 hours | Serves 4

- 3 tablespoons olive oil
- 4 cloves garlic, minced
- 3 shallot cloves, minced
- 8 ounces (227 g) mushrooms, diced
- 1 (28-ounce / 794-g) can diced tomatoes, with the juice
- ¾ cup white wine
- 2 tablespoons dried oregano
- ½ tablespoon dried basil
- ½ teaspoon black pepper
- 1 teaspoon paprika
- ¼ teaspoon red pepper flakes
- 3 pounds (1.4 kg) mussels

1. Warm the olive oil in a large sauté pan over medium-high heat. Add the garlic, shallots, and mushrooms, cooking for 2 to 3 minutes until the garlic is lightly browned and fragrant. Transfer everything from the pan into the slow cooker.
2. Add the tomatoes and white wine to the cooker, then season with oregano, basil, black pepper, paprika, and red pepper flakes.
3. Cover and cook on low for 4 to 5 hours, or on high for 2 to 3 hours, until the mushrooms are tender when pierced with a fork.
4. While the mixture cooks, clean and debeard the mussels, discarding any that are already open.
5. Once the mushroom mixture is finished, turn the slow cooker to high. Add the mussels, secure the lid, and cook for another 30 minutes.
6. To serve, ladle mussels and plenty of broth into bowls, discarding any that failed to open. Serve hot alongside crusty bread for dipping into the sauce.

Crab Claws with Garlic

Prep time: 10 minutes | Cook time: 5½ hours | Serves 6 to 8

- 1 cup (2 sticks) unsalted butter
- ½ cup olive oil
- 10 cloves garlic, sliced
- 2 tablespoons Old Bay seasoning
- 2 cups dry white wine or vermouth
- 1 lemon, thinly sliced
- 3 to 4 pounds (1.4 to 1.8 kg) cooked crab legs and claws, cracked

1. Put the butter, oil, garlic, seasoning, wine, and lemon in the insert of a 5- to 7-quart slow cooker.
2. Cover and cook on low for 4 hours. Add the crab, spoon the sauce over the crab, and cook for an additional 1½ hours, turning the crab in the sauce during cooking.
3. Serve the crab from the cooker set on warm.

Cod with Miso Glaze

Prep time: 15 minutes | Cook time: 5 hours | Serves 6

½ cup white miso paste

- ¼ cup rice wine (mirin)
- ¼ firmly packed light brown sugar
- 1 teaspoon rice vinegar
- 1 ½ cups water
- 2 pounds (907 g) black cod (if unavailable, use fresh cod, halibut, sea bass, or salmon)
- 6 green onions, finely chopped, using the white and tender green parts
- ¼ cup toasted sesame seeds for garnish

1. Combine the miso, rice wine, sugar, rice vinegar, and water in the insert of a 5- to 7-quart slow cooker.
2. Cover and cook on low for 4 hours. Add the cod, spooning the sauce over the top. Cover and cook for an additional 30 to 45 minutes.
3. Remove the cod from the slow-cooker insert and cover with aluminum foil to keep warm. Pour the sauce in a saucepan. Bring to a boil and reduce by half until it begins to look syrupy, about 15 to 20 minutes. Add the green onions to the sauce.
4. Serve each piece of cod in a pool of the sauce, and sprinkle each serving with sesame seeds. Serve any additional sauce on the side.

Shrimp with Marinara Sauce

Prep time: 15 minutes | Cook time: 6 to 7 hours | Serves 4

- 1 (15-ounce / 425-g) can diced tomatoes, with the juice
- 1 (6-ounce / 170-g) can tomato paste
- 1 clove garlic, minced
- 2 tablespoons minced fresh flat-leaf parsley
- ½ teaspoon dried basil
- 1 teaspoon dried oregano
- 1 teaspoon garlic powder
- 1½ teaspoons sea salt
- ¼ teaspoon black pepper
- 1 pound (454 g) cooked shrimp, peeled and deveined
- 2 cups hot cooked spaghetti or linguine, for serving
- ½ cup grated Parmesan cheese, for serving

1. Use the butter to grease the inside of the slow cooker.
2. In a small bowl, whisk the eggs, milk, dill, salt, and a few twists of black pepper until well combined.
3. Arrange one-third of the potatoes in an even layer on the bottom of the slow cooker, then add one-third of the salmon. Pour over one-third of the egg mixture. Repeat the layering process with the rest of the potatoes, salmon, and egg mixture.
4. Cover with the lid and cook on low for 8 hours or overnight.

Mahi-Mahi with Tropical Fruit Salsa and Lentils

Prep time: 30 minutes | Cook time: 6 hours | Serves 6

- 1¼ cups vegetable or chicken stock
- 1 cup orange juice
- ¾ cup orange lentils
- ½ cup finely diced carrot
- ¼ cup finely diced red onion
- ¼ cup finely diced celery

Salsa:

- ¾ cup finely diced pineapple
- ¾ cup finely diced mango
- ½ cup finely diced strawberries
- ¼ cup finely diced red onion
- 1 tablespoon honey
- 6 (4- to-5-ounce / 113- to 142-g) mahi-mahi fillets
- Sea salt
- Black pepper
- 1 teaspoon lemon juice
- 2 tablespoons chopped fresh mint (or 2 teaspoons dried)
- 2 tablespoons orange juice
- 1 tablespoon lime juice
- ¼ teaspoon salt

1. Combine the stock, orange juice, lentils, carrot, onion, celery, and honey in the slow cooker.
2. Cover and cook on low for 5 to 5½ hours, or until the lentils are tender.
3. Place 1 sheet of parchment paper over the lentils in the slow cooker. Season mahi-mahi lightly with salt and black pepper and place it on the parchment (skin-side down, if you have not removed the skin). Replace the lid and continue to cook on low for 25 minutes or until the mahi-mahi is opaque in the center. Remove the fish by lifting out the parchment paper and putting it on a plate.
4. Stir the lemon juice into the lentils and season with salt and pepper.

Make the Salsa:

5. While the fish is cooking, combine the pineapple, mango, strawberries, red onion, mint, orange juice, lime juice, and salt into a big jar. Combine and chill to give the flavours a chance to blend.
6. To serve, place about ½ cup of hot lentils on a plate and top with a mahimahi fillet and ⅓ cup of salsa.

Gulf Shrimp Gumbo

Prep time: 35 minutes | Cook time: 5 hours | Serves 6

- ½ pound (227 g) bacon strips, chopped
- 3 celery ribs, chopped
- 1 medium onion, chopped
- 1 medium green pepper, chopped
- 2 garlic cloves, minced
- 2 (8-ounce / 227-g) bottles clam juice
- 1 (14½-ounce / 411-g) can diced tomatoes, undrained
- 2 tablespoons Worcestershire sauce
- 1 teaspoon kosher salt
- 1 teaspoon dried marjoram
- 2 pounds (907 g) uncooked large shrimp, peeled and deveined
- 2½ cups frozen sliced okra, thawed
- Hot cooked rice

1. In a large skillet, cook bacon over medium heat until crisp. Remove to paper towels with a slotted spoon; drain, reserving 2 tablespoons drippings. Saute the celery, onion, green pepper and garlic in drippings until tender.
2. Transfer to a 4-quart slow cooker. Stir in the bacon, clam juice, tomatoes, Worcestershire sauce, salt and marjoram. Cover and cook on low for 4 hours.
3. Stir in shrimp and okra. Cover and cook 1 hour longer or until shrimp turn pink and okra is heated through. Serve with rice.

Poached Salmon of Provence

Prep time: 15 minutes | Cook time: 1½ to 2 hours | Serves 6

- 3 pounds (1.4 kg) salmon fillets
- ½ cup dry white wine or vermouth
- 4 cloves garlic, peeled
- 1½ teaspoons finely chopped fresh rosemary
- 2 teaspoons finely chopped fresh thyme leaves
- 2 teaspoons finely chopped fresh tarragon
- ½ cup olive oil
- 1 (28- to 32-ounce / 794- to 907-g) can plum tomatoes, drained
- ½ cup heavy cream
- Salt and freshly ground black pepper

1. Set the salmon in the insert of a 5- to 7-quart slow cooker, then pour the white wine over the top.
2. Combine the garlic, rosemary, thyme, tarragon, oil, and tomatoes in a food processor and blend until smooth. Spoon this mixture across the salmon so it is well coated.
3. Cover the cooker and let it cook on high for 1½ to 2 hours, or until the fish is opaque and flakes easily.
4. Lift the salmon carefully onto a serving platter and peel away the skin. Transfer the cooking sauce to a saucepan, bring it to a boil, and let it reduce by about ¼ cup. Stir in the heavy cream, seasoning with salt and pepper to taste.
5. Serve the salmon with some of the sauce spooned over it, and offer the rest alongside.

Salmon with Lemon Dijon and Dill Barley

Prep time: 15 minutes | Cook time: 2 hours | Serves 6

- 1 medium yellow onion, diced
- 2 teaspoons garlic, minced
- 2 teaspoons olive oil
- 2 cups vegetable or chicken stock
- 1 cup quick-cooking barley
- 1 tablespoon minced fresh dill weed
- 1½ pounds (680 g) salmon fillets
- Sea salt
- Black pepper

Lemon-Dijon Sauce:

- ⅓ cup Dijon mustard
- 3 tablespoons olive oil
- 3 tablespoons fresh lemon juice
- ⅓ cup plain Greek yoghurt
- 1 clove garlic, minced

1. Combine the onion, garlic, and oil in a microwave-safe bowl. Heat in the microwave on 70 percent power for 4 to 5 minutes, stirring occasionally. Put into the slow cooker.
2. Add the stock, barley, and dill weed to the slow cooker and stir.
3. Season the salmon fillets with salt and pepper, and gently place them on top of the barley mixture.
4. Cover and cook on low for about 2 hours, until the salmon and barley are cooked through.

Make the Lemon-Dijon Sauce:

5. In a small bowl, whisk together the Dijon mustard, olive oil, lemon juice, Greek yoghurt, and garlic. Set aside and allow the flavours to blend.
6. To serve, place some barley on a plate and top with a salmon fillet. Spoon the lemon-Dijon sauce over the top of the salmon.

Cioppino with Scallops and Crab

Prep time: 15 minutes | Cook time: 7 hours | Serves 4

- Cooking oil spray
- 1 medium yellow onion, finely chopped
- 4 cloves garlic, minced
- 1 (15-ounce / 425-g) can diced tomatoes, with the juice
- 1 (10-ounce / 283-g) can diced tomatoes with green chiles
- 2 cups seafood stock
- 1 cup red wine
- 3 tablespoons chopped fresh basil
- 2 bay leaves
- 1 pound (454 g) cooked crab meat, shredded
- 1½ pounds (680 g) scallops
- Sea salt
- Black pepper
- ¼ cup fresh flat-leaf parsley, for garnish

1. Coat a large sauté pan with cooking oil spray and heat over medium-high heat. Add the onion and sauté for about 5 minutes, until softened.
2. Add the garlic and sauté until golden and fragrant, about 2 minutes.
3. Transfer the onion and garlic to the slow cooker, and add the tomatoes, tomatoes with green chiles, stock, wine, basil, and bay leaves. Cover and cook on low for 6 hours.
4. About 30 minutes before the cooking time is completed, add the crab meat and scallops. Cover and cook on high for 30 minutes. The seafood will turn opaque. Season to taste with salt and pepper. Serve hot, garnished with parsley.

Halibut with Lemon Garlic Butter

Prep time: 15 minutes | Cook time: 5 hours | Serves 6

- 1 cup (2 sticks) unsalted butter
- ½ cup olive oil
- 6 cloves garlic, sliced
- 1 teaspoon sweet paprika
- ½ cup lemon juice
- Grated zest of 1 lemon
- ¼ cup finely chopped fresh chives
- 2 to 3 pounds (907 g to 1.4 kg) halibut fillets
- ½ cup finely chopped fresh Italian parsley

1. Combine the butter, oil, garlic, paprika, lemon juice, zest, and chives in the insert of a 5- to 7-quart slow cooker and stir to combine. Cover and cook on low for 4 hours.
2. Add the halibut to the pot, spooning the sauce over the halibut. Cover and cook for an additional 40 minutes, until the halibut is cooked through and opaque.
3. Sprinkle the parsley evenly over the fish, and serve immediately.

Barbecued Scallops and Shrimp with Spice

Prep time: 20 minutes | Cook time: 1 hour | Serves 2

- ½ teaspoon paprika
- ½ teaspoon garlic powder
- ¼ teaspoon onion powder
- ¼ teaspoon cayenne pepper
- ¼ teaspoon dried oregano
- ¼ teaspoon dried thyme
- ½ teaspoon sea salt
- ½ teaspoon black pepper
- 2 cloves garlic, minced
- ½ cup olive oil
- ¼ cup Worcestershire sauce
- 1 tablespoon hot pepper sauce (like Tabasco)
- Juice of 1 lemon
- 1 pound (454 g) scallops
- 1 pound (454 g) large shrimp, unpeeled
- 1 green onion, finely chopped

1. Combine the paprika, garlic powder, onion powder, cayenne pepper, oregano, thyme, ½ teaspoon salt, and ¼ teaspoon black pepper.
2. Combine the paprika blend, garlic, olive oil, Worcestershire sauce, hot pepper sauce, and lemon juice in the slow cooker. Season with salt and pepper.
3. Cover and cook on high for 30 minutes or until hot.
4. Rinse the scallops and shrimp, and drain.
5. Spoon one-half of the sauce from the slow cooker into a glass measuring cup.
6. Place the scallops and shrimp in the slow cooker with the remaining sauce. Drizzle with the sauce in the measuring cup, and stir to coat.
7. Cover and cook on high for 30 minutes, until the scallops and shrimp are opaque.
8. Turn the heat to warm for serving. Sprinkle with the chopped green onion to serve.

Chapter 6 Fish and Seafood

South-of-the-Border Halibut

Prep time: 10 minutes | Cook time: 3½ hours | Serves 6

- 3 cups prepared medium-hot salsa
- 2 tablespoons fresh lime juice
- 1 teaspoon ground cumin
- 2 to 3 pounds (907 g to 1.4 kg) halibut fillets
- 1½ cup finely shredded Monterey Jack cheese (or Pepper Jack for a spicy topping)

1. In the insert of a 5- to 7-quart slow cooker, mix together the salsa, lime juice, and cumin. Cover with the lid and cook on low for 2 hours.
2. Add the halibut to the cooker, spooning some of the sauce over the fish. Sprinkle the cheese evenly on top. Cover again and cook for another 30 to 45 minutes.
3. Carefully remove the halibut from the cooker and serve it over a bed of the sauce.

Acadiana Shrimp Barbecue

Prep time: 15 minutes | Cook time: 4 hours | Serves 6 to 8

- 1 cup (2 sticks) unsalted butter
- ¼ cup olive oil
- 8 cloves garlic, sliced
- 2 teaspoons dried oregano
- 1 teaspoon dried thyme
- ½ teaspoon freshly ground black pepper
- Pinch of cayenne pepper
- 2 teaspoons sweet paprika
- ¼ cup Worcestershire sauce
- ¼ cup lemon juice
- 3 pounds (1.4 kg) large shrimp, peeled and deveined
- ½ cup finely chopped fresh Italian parsley

1. Place the butter, oil, garlic, oregano, thyme, pepper, cayenne, paprika, Worcestershire sauce, and lemon juice into the insert of a 5- to 7-quart slow cooker. Cover and cook on low for 4 hours.
2. Switch the cooker to high, add the shrimp, and toss them in the butter sauce. Cover again and cook for 5 to 10 minutes, until the shrimp turn pink.
3. Transfer the shrimp to a large serving bowl, pour the sauce over the top, sprinkle with parsley, and serve immediately.

Cajun Shrimp

Prep time: 15 minutes | Cook time: 3½ to 7 hours | Serves 6

- ¾ pound (340 g) andouille sausage, cut into ½-inch rounds (you may substitute Kiel-basa if you cannot find andouille sausage)
- 1 red onion, sliced into wedges
- 2 garlic cloves, minced
- 2 celery stalks, coarsely chopped
- 1 red or green bell pepper, coarsely chopped
- 2 tablespoons all-purpose flour
- 1 (28-ounce / 794-g) can diced tomatoes, with their juice
- ¼ teaspoon cayenne pepper
- Coarse sea salt
- ½ pound (227 g) large shrimp, peeled and deveined
- 2 cups fresh okra, sliced (you may substitute frozen and thawed, if necessary)

1. Place the sausage, onion, garlic, celery, and bell pepper in the slow cooker. Sprinkle the flour over the top and toss everything together to coat.
2. Pour in the tomatoes and ½ cup water, then season with cayenne pepper and a little salt.
3. Cover and cook on high for 3½ hours or on low for 7 hours, until the vegetables have softened.
4. Add the shrimp and okra, cover again, and cook until the shrimp turn opaque—about 30 minutes on high or 1 hour on low. Serve hot.

Pacifica Sweet-Hot Salmon

Prep time: 10 minutes | Cook time: 1½ hours | Serves 6

- 3 pounds (1.4 kg) salmon fillets
- ½ cup Colman's English mustard
- ¼ cup honey
- 2 tablespoons finely chopped fresh dill

1. Put the salmon into the insert of a 5- to 7-quart slow cooker. In a small bowl, mix together the mustard, honey, and dill until blended.
2. Spread this mixture evenly over the salmon.
3. Cover with the lid and cook on high for 1½ hours, or until the salmon is fully cooked.
4. Serve the salmon straight from the slow cooker, topped with some of the sauce.

Creole Crayfish

Prep time: 15 minutes | Cook time: 3 to 8 hours | Serves 2

- 1½ cups diced celery
- 1 large yellow onion, chopped
- 2 small bell peppers, any colours, chopped
- 1 (8-ounce / 227-g) can tomato sauce
- 1 (28-ounce / 794-g) can whole tomatoes, broken up, with the juice
- 1 clove garlic, minced
- 1 teaspoon sea salt
- ¼ teaspoon black pepper
- 6 drops hot pepper sauce (like Tabasco)
- 1 pound (454 g) precooked crayfish meat

1. Put the celery, onion, and bell peppers into the slow cooker. Add the tomato sauce, tomatoes, and garlic, then season with salt and pepper and pour in the hot sauce.
2. Cover with the lid and cook on high for 3 to 4 hours, or set to low for 6 to 8 hours.
3. Add the crayfish about 30 minutes before the end of the cooking time.
4. Serve the dish hot.

Sea Bass Tagine

Prep time: 25 minutes | Cook time: 6 to 7½ hours | Serves 6

- 2 pounds (907 g) sea bass fillets
- ½ cup olive oil
- Grated zest of 1 lemon
- ¼ cup lemon juice
- 1 teaspoon sweet paprika
- ½ cup finely chopped fresh cilantro
- 2 cloves garlic, chopped
- 1 medium onion, finely chopped
- 1 teaspoon ground cumin
- ½ teaspoon saffron threads, crushed
- 1 (28- to 32-ounce / 794- to 907-g) can crushed tomatoes, with their juice
- 6 medium Yukon gold potatoes, quartered
- 1 teaspoon salt
- ½ teaspoon freshly ground black pepper
- ½ cup finely chopped fresh Italian parsley

1. Place the fish into a resealable plastic bag.
2. In a small bowl, whisk together ¼ cup oil, the lemon zest, lemon juice, paprika, and cilantro. Pour this marinade over the fish, seal the bag, and refrigerate for at least 1 hour or up to 4 hours.
3. Heat the remaining ¼ cup oil in a large skillet over medium-high heat. Add the garlic, onion, cumin, and saffron, and sauté for 5 to 7 minutes, until the onion has softened.
4. Stir in the tomatoes, then transfer the mixture to the insert of a 5- to 7-quart slow cooker. Place the potatoes in the insert, season with salt and pepper, and toss to coat. Cover and cook on low for 5 to 6 hours, until the potatoes are nearly tender.
5. Pour the marinade into the slow cooker and stir gently to mix it with the potatoes and sauce. Arrange the fish on top, spoon some of the sauce over it, and cook for 1 to 1½ hours, until the sea bass is opaque and cooked through.
6. Sprinkle parsley evenly over the fish and serve right away, making sure to include some potatoes and sauce with each portion.

Potato-Crusted Sea Bass

Prep time: 15 minutes | Cook time: 1½ hours | Serves 6

- 1 cup (2 sticks) unsalted butter, melted and cooled
- ½ cup fresh lemon juice
- Grated zest of 1 lemon
- 2 cloves garlic, minced
- 8 tablespoons olive oil
- 2 tablespoons Old Bay seasoning
- 2 to 3 pounds (907 g to 1.4 kg) sea bass fillets, cut to fit the slow-cooker insert
- 6 medium Yukon gold potatoes, cut into ¼-inch-thick slices

1. In a small bowl, mix together the butter, lemon juice, zest, garlic, and 2 tablespoons of olive oil. In a separate large bowl, combine the remaining 6 tablespoons of oil with the seasoning.
2. Brush the sea bass with some of the butter mixture and set it aside. Toss the potatoes in the seasoned oil, then pour half of the butter mixture into the insert of a 5- to 7-quart slow cooker.
3. Layer half the potatoes in the bottom of the insert. Place the sea bass on top, drizzle with half of the remaining butter mixture, then cover with the rest of the potatoes. Finish by spooning the remaining butter mixture over the top.
4. Cover and cook on high for 1½ hours, until the potatoes start to turn golden and the fish is opaque and cooked through. Remove the lid and continue cooking uncovered for another 15 to 20 minutes.
5. Serve right away.

Swordfish with Citrus

Prep time: 15 minutes | Cook time: 1½ hours | Serves 2

- Nonstick cooking oil spray
- 1½ pounds (680 g) swordfish fillets
- Sea salt
- Black pepper
- 1 yellow onion, chopped
- 5 tablespoons chopped fresh flat-leaf parsley
- 1 tablespoon olive oil
- 2 teaspoons lemon zest
- 2 teaspoons orange zest
- Orange and lemon slices, for garnish
- Fresh parsley sprigs, for garnish

1. Coat the interior of the slow cooker crock with nonstick cooking oil spray.
2. Season the fish fillets with salt and pepper. Place the fish in the slow cooker.
3. Distribute the onion, parsley, olive oil, lemon zest, and orange zest over fish.
4. Cover and cook on low for 1½ hours.
5. Serve hot, garnished with orange and lemon slices and sprigs of fresh parsley.

Catalan Seafood Stew

Prep time: 20 minutes | Cook time: 7 hours | Serves 6 to 8

- ½ cup extra-virgin olive oil
- 2 medium onions, finely chopped
- 2 medium red bell peppers, seeded and finely chopped
- 6 cloves garlic, minced
- 1 teaspoon saffron threads, crushed
- 1 teaspoon hot paprika
- 1 cup finely chopped Spanish chorizo or soppressata salami
- 1 (28- to 32-ounce / 794- to 907-g) can crushed tomatoes
- 2 cups clam juice
- 1 cup chicken broth
- 2 pounds (907 g) firm-fleshed fish, such as halibut, monkfish, cod, or sea bass fillets, cut into 1-inch chunks
- 1½ pounds (680 g) littleneck clams
- ½ cup finely chopped fresh Italian parsley

1. Heat the oil in a large skillet over medium-high heat. Add the onions, bell peppers, garlic, saffron, paprika, and chorizo and sauté until the vegetables are softened, 5 to 7 minutes. Add the tomatoes and transfer the contents of the skillet to the insert of a 5- to 7-quart slow cooker. Add the clam juice and broth and stir to combine.
2. Cover and cook on low for 6 hours. Add the fish and clams to the slow-cooker insert, spooning some of the sauce over the fish and pushing the clams under the sauce.
3. Cover and cook for an additional 45 to 50 minutes, until the clams have opened and the fish is cooked through and opaque. Discard any clams that haven't opened.
4. Sprinkle the parsley over the stew and serve immediately.

Poached Salmon Cakes in White Wine Butter Sauce

Prep time: 15 minutes | Cook time: 5 hours | Serves 6

White Wine Butter Sauce:

- ½ cup (1 stick) unsalted butter
- 1 teaspoon Old Bay seasoning
- 2 cloves garlic, sliced
- 2½ cups white wine or vermouth

Salmon Cakes:

- 4 cups cooked salmon, flaked
- 1 (6-ounce / 170-g) jar marinated artichoke hearts, drained and coarsely chopped
- 1 cup fresh bread crumbs
- ½ cup freshly grated Parmigiano-Reggiano cheese
- 1 large egg, beaten
- ½ teaspoon freshly ground black pepper

1. Add all of the sauce ingredients to the insert of a 5- to 7-quart slow cooker and stir well. Cover with the lid and cook on low for 4 hours.
2. In a large bowl, combine all the salmon cake ingredients and mix until blended. Shape the mixture into 2-inch cakes, then place them gently into the simmering sauce, spooning some of the sauce over the tops.
3. Cover again and cook for 1 more hour, until the cakes are firm and tender. Remove them carefully to a serving platter.
4. Strain the sauce through a fine-mesh sieve into a saucepan, bring it to a boil, and reduce by half.
5. Spoon the sauce over the salmon cakes to serve, or offer it separately on the side.

Traditional Coconut Seafood Laksa

Prep time: 30 minutes | Cook time: 2½ hours | Serves 6 to 8

- 2 tablespoons virgin coconut oil or extra-virgin olive oil
- 1 small onion, chopped
- 4 Thai bird chiles
- 1 (2-inch) piece fresh ginger, peeled and grated
- 1 (1-inch) piece fresh turmeric, peeled and grated
- 1 lemongrass stalk, tough outer leaves discarded, inner bulb chopped
- ¼ cup fresh cilantro
- 1 tablespoon tamarind paste
- ½ teaspoon ground cumin
- ½ teaspoon paprika
- 2 teaspoon coarse salt
- 2 cups unsweetened coconut milk
- 2 cups boiling water
- 4 kaffir lime leaves
- 2 teaspoon fish sauce
- 1 pound (454 g) medium shrimp, peeled and deveined (shells rinsed and reserved)
- 2 pounds (907 g) small mussels, scrubbed
- ¾ pound (340 g) firm fish fillet, such as halibut or cod, cut into 1-inch pieces
- 8 ounces (227 g) rice noodles
- Lime wedges, cubed firm tofu, sliced scallions, sliced Thai bird chiles, cilantro, and chili oil, for serving

1. Preheat a 7-quart slow cooker.
2. Heat oil in a saucepan over medium. Add onion and cook until translucent, about 5 minutes. Add chiles, ginger, turmeric, lemongrass, cilantro, tamarind paste, cumin, paprika, and salt. Cook until fragrant, about 2 more minutes. Remove from heat and let cool. Transfer spice mixture to a food processor and puree to a thick paste.
3. Combine laksa paste, coconut milk, the boiling water, lime leaves, fish sauce, and shrimp shells in the slow cooker. Cover and cook on low for 2 hours (we prefer this recipe on low).
4. Strain liquid through a medium sieve into a bowl, pressing down on solids; return broth to slow cooker (discard solids). Add shrimp and mussels, and cook on low 20 minutes. Add fish and cook until shrimp is completely cooked through, fish is firm, and mussels open, about 10 minutes.
5. Meanwhile, prepare noodles according to package instructions.
6. To serve, divide noodles among bowls. Add broth and seafood, and top with tofu, scallions, chiles, and cilantro. Serve with lime wedges and chili oil.

Garlic Tilapia

Prep time: 5 minutes | Cook time: 2 hours | Serves 4

- 2 tablespoons butter, at room temperature
- 2 cloves garlic, minced
- 2 teaspoons minced fresh flat-leaf parsley
- 4 tilapia fillets
- Sea salt
- Black pepper

1. In a small bowl, stir together the butter, garlic, and parsley until blended.
2. Lay a large sheet of aluminum foil on the counter and set the fillets in the center.
3. Season the fish well with salt and pepper.
4. Spread the butter mixture evenly over the fillets.
5. Fold the foil around the fish, sealing tightly and crimping the edges to form a packet. Place the packet in the slow cooker, cover, and cook on high for 2 hours. Serve hot.

Miso Poached Salmon

Prep time: 10 minutes | Cook time: 1½ hours | Serves 8

- 3 pounds (1.4 kg) salmon fillets
- 3 tablespoons white miso
- 3 tablespoons honey
- ¼ cup rice wine (mirin) or dry sherry
- 2 teaspoons freshly grated ginger

1. place the salmon in the insert of a 5- to 7-quart slow cooker.
2. Combine the miso, honey, rice wine, and ginger in a mixing bowl and stir.
3. Pour the sauce over the salmon in the slow cooker. Cover and cook on high for 1½ hours, until the salmon is cooked through and registers 165ºF (74ºC) on an instant-read thermometer inserted in the center of a thick fillet.
4. Carefully remove the salmon from the slow-cooker insert with a large spatula. Remove the skin from the underside of the salmon (if necessary) and arrange the salmon on a serving platter.
5. Strain the sauce through a fine-mesh sieve into a saucepan. Boil the sauce, reduce it to a syrupy consistency, and serve with the salmon.

Beantown Scallops

Prep time: 10 minutes | Cook time: 4½ hours | Serves 6

- 1 cup (2 sticks) unsalted butter
- 2 tablespoons olive oil
- 2 cloves garlic, minced
- 2 teaspoons sweet paprika
- ¼ cup dry sherry
- 2 pounds (907 g) dry-pack sea scallops
- ½ cup finely chopped fresh Italian parsley

1. Place the butter, oil, garlic, paprika, and sherry into the insert of a 5- to 7-quart slow cooker.
2. Cover and cook on low for 4 hours. Switch the setting to high, add the scallops, and toss them in the butter sauce. Cover again and cook for 30 to 40 minutes, until the scallops turn opaque.
3. Remove the scallops along with the sauce from the cooker, transfer to a serving platter, sprinkle with parsley, and serve immediately.

Barley Risotto with Shrimp and Artichokes

Prep time: 15 minutes | Cook time: 3 hours | Serves 4

- 3 cups seafood stock (or chicken stock)
- 1 teaspoon olive oil
- 1 yellow onion, chopped
- 3 cloves garlic, minced
- 1 (9-ounce / 255-g) package frozen artichoke hearts, thawed and quartered
- 1 cup uncooked pearl barley
- Black pepper
- 1 pound (454 g) shrimp, peeled and deveined
- 2 ounces (57 g) Parmesan or Pecorino Romano cheese, grated
- 2 teaspoons lemon zest
- 4 ounces (113 g) fresh baby spinach

1. Bring the stock to a boil in a medium saucepan. Remove from the heat and set aside.
2. In a nonstick medium skillet over medium-high heat, heat the olive oil. Add the onion and sauté until tender, about 5 minutes. Add the garlic and sauté for 1 more minute.
3. Transfer the onion and garlic to the slow cooker and add the artichoke hearts and barley. Season with some pepper. Stir in the seafood stock.
4. Cover and cook on high for 3 hours, or until the barley is tender and the liquid is just about all absorbed.
5. About 15 minutes before the cooking time is completed, stir in the shrimp and grated cheese. Cover and continue to cook on high for another 10 minutes, or until the shrimp are opaque.
6. Add the lemon zest and fold in the baby spinach, stirring until it's wilted, about 1 minute.
7. Divide the risotto among the serving bowls and serve hot.

Low Country Seafood Boil

Prep time: 15 minutes | Cook time: 6 hours | Serves 8

8 medium red potatoes

- 2 large, sweet onions, such as Vidalia, quartered
- 2 pounds (907 g) smoked sausage, cut into 3-inch pieces
- 1 (3-ounce / 85-g) package seafood boil seasoning
- 1 (12-ounce / 340-g) bottle pale ale beer
- 10 cups water
- 4 ears of corn, halved
- 2 pounds (907 g) medium raw shrimp, shelled and deveined
- Cocktail sauce, for serving
- Hot sauce, for serving
- ½ cup melted butter, for serving
- 1 large lemon, cut into wedges, for garnish

1. Place the potatoes, onions, smoked sausage, seafood boil seasoning, beer, and water into the slow cooker. Stir everything together, then cover and cook for 6 hours, or until the potatoes are fork-tender.
2. Roughly 45 minutes before serving, add the corn. Cover again and cook for 25 minutes. Stir in the shrimp, cover, and cook just until they turn pink and opaque.
3. Drain the contents of the slow cooker, discarding the liquid, and serve the seafood with cocktail sauce, hot sauce, melted butter, and lemon wedges on the side.

Tender Halibut with Tangy Eggplant Ginger Relish

Prep time: 25 minutes | Cook time: 4 hours | Serves 4

- 4 medium Japanese eggplants (or 2 large eggplants), cut into ½-inch cubes
- ¼ cup coarse salt
- ¼ cup extra-virgin olive oil
- 2 onions, diced
- 3 garlic cloves, minced
- 1 (1-inch) piece fresh ginger, peeled and finely grated
- 2 kaffir lime leaves
- 2 teaspoon brown sugar
- 1 tablespoon rice vinegar
- ¼ cup fresh lime juice
- 1 cup packed fresh cilantro, finely chopped
- 1 pound (454 g) halibut, cut into 1-inch pieces
- ½ cup unsweetened flaked coconut, toasted, for garnish

1. Combine eggplant and salt in a colander set over a bowl; let stand about 1 hour. Rinse well and pat dry.
2. Preheat a 5- to 6-quart slow cooker.
3. Heat 2 tablespoons oil in a large skillet over medium. Add onions and sauté until deeply golden, about 15 minutes. Add garlic and ginger, and cook 2 more minutes. Add eggplants and cook just until hot. Transfer vegetables to the slow cooker.
4. Add remaining 2 tablespoons oil, the lime leaves, brown sugar, vinegar, and lime juice to slow cooker. Cover and cook on low until very soft but not mushy, about 4 hours (or on high for 2 hours).
5. Stir in cilantro. Nestle fish on top of eggplant mixture and cook on low until cooked through, about 20 minutes (or on high for 10 minutes). Serve relish topped with halibut and sprinkled with toasted coconut.

Classic Bouillabaisse

Prep time: 25 minutes | Cook time: 7 to 9 hours | Serves 6 to 8

- ¼ cup extra-virgin olive oil
- 3 leeks, cleaned and coarsely chopped, using the white and tender green parts
- 4 cloves garlic, sliced
- 1 bulb fennel, ends trimmed, coarsely chopped
- Grated zest of 1 orange
- 1 teaspoon dried thyme
- 1 teaspoon saffron threads, crushed
- Pinch of cayenne pepper
- 1 (28- to 32-ounce / 794- to 907-g) can crushed tomatoes, with their juice
- ½ cup white wine or dry vermouth
- 3 cups clam juice
- 1 cup chicken broth
- ½ pound (227 g) littleneck clams
- ½ pound (227 g) mussels
- 3 pounds (1.4 kg) thick-fleshed fish, cut into 1-inch chunks
- ½ cup finely chopped fresh Italian parsley

1. Heat the oil in a large skillet over medium-high heat. Add the leeks, garlic, fennel, zest, thyme, saffron, and cayenne and sauté until the vegetables are softened, about 2 minutes. Add the tomatoes and wine and cook down for 10 minutes, to concentrate the flavours. Transfer the mixture to the insert of a 5- to 7-quart slow cooker.
2. Add the clam juice and broth to the slow-cooker insert and stir to combine. Cover and cook on low for 6 to 8 hours. Remove the cover and place the clams and mussels in the sauce.
3. Place the fish on top of the shellfish and spoon the sauce over the top of the fish. Cover and cook on high for 45 minutes, until the fish is cooked through and opaque and the clams and mussels have opened.
4. Discard any clams and mussels that haven't opened. Sprinkle with the parsley and serve immediately.

Chapter 7

Stews and Soups

Chapter 7 Stews and Soups

Creamy Tomato Soup

Prep time: 20 minutes | Cook time: 1½ hours | Serves 6

- 1 (26-ounce / 737-g) can condensed tomato soup, plus 6 ounces (170 g) water to equal 1 quart
- ½ teaspoon salt (optional)
- Half a stick butter
- 8 tablespoons flour
- 1 quart milk (whole or reduced-fat)

1. Place the tomato soup, butter, and salt (if using) into the slow cooker and stir until well blended.
2. Cover with the lid and cook on high for 1 hour.
3. In a 2-quart microwave-safe container, whisk together the flour and 1 cup of milk until most of the lumps are gone. Gradually whisk in the rest of the milk until only small lumps remain.
4. Microwave the flour-milk mixture on high for 3 minutes, then remove and stir until smooth. Return to the microwave and cook for another 3 minutes on high.
5. Slowly add the thickened milk into the hot soup in the slow cooker, stirring as you pour.
6. Heat the combined mixture thoroughly in the slow cooker for 10 to 15 minutes before serving.

Vegetable Stew with Curry

Prep time: 15 minutes | Cook time: 7 to 8 hours | Serves 6

- 1 tablespoon extra-virgin olive oil
- 4 cups coconut milk
- 1 cup diced pumpkin
- 1 cup cauliflower florets
- 1 red bell pepper, diced
- 1 zucchini, diced
- 1 sweet onion, chopped
- 2 teaspoons grated fresh ginger
- 2 teaspoons minced garlic
- 1 tablespoon curry powder
- 2 cups shredded spinach
- 1 avocado, diced, for garnish

1. Lightly grease the insert of the slow cooker with the olive oil.
2. Add the coconut milk, pumpkin, cauliflower, bell pepper, zucchini, onion, ginger, garlic, and curry powder.
3. Cover and cook on low for 7 to 8 hours.
4. Stir in the spinach.
5. Garnish each bowl with a spoonful of avocado and serve.

Savoury Sesame-Infused Miso Soup with Tofu and Shrimp

Prep time: 20 minutes | Cook time: 3 to 3½ hours | Serves 8

- 2 tablespoons vegetable oil
- 1 clove garlic, minced
- 1 teaspoon freshly grated ginger
- 8 ounces (227 g) shiitake mushrooms, stems removed, caps sliced
- ¼ cup light miso paste
- 6 cups vegetable or chicken broth
- 2 teaspoons soy sauce
- 1 pound (454 g) firm tofu, cut into ½-inch cubes
- 1 pound (454 g) medium shrimp, peeled and deveined, tails removed
- 6 green onions, finely chopped
- Toasted sesame oil for drizzling
- Toasted sesame seeds, for garnish

1. Heat the vegetable oil in a large skillet over high heat. Add the garlic and ginger and sauté until they are fragrant, about 1 minute. Add the mushrooms and toss with the garlic and ginger.
2. Transfer the contents of the skillet to the insert of a 5- to 7-quart slow cooker. Stir in the miso, broth, and soy sauce.
3. Cover and cook on high for 2½ to 3 hours. Add the tofu and shrimp, cover, turn the cooker to low, and cook until the shrimp are pink and cooked through, about 30 minutes.
4. Add the green onions to the soup and serve drizzled with the sesame oil and garnished with sesame seeds.

Beef and Sausage Soup

Prep time: 25 minutes | Cook time: 8 to 10 hours | Serves 4 to 6

- 1 pound (454 g) ground beef
- 1 pound (454 g) Polish sausage, sliced
- ½ teaspoon seasoned salt
- ¼ teaspoon dried oregano
- ¼ teaspoon dried basil
- 1 package dry onion soup mix
- 6 cups boiling water
- 1 (16-ounce / 454-g) can diced tomatoes
- 1 tablespoon soy sauce
- ½ cup sliced celery
- ¼ cup chopped celery leaves
- 1 cup pared, sliced carrots
- 1 cup macaroni, uncooked

1. Brown ground beef and sausage in skillet. Drain. Place in slow cooker.
2. Add seasoned salt, oregano, basil, and onion soup mix to cooker.
3. Stir in boiling water, tomatoes, and soy sauce.
4. Add celery, celery leaves, and carrots. Stir well.
5. Cover. Cook on low 8 to 10 hours.
6. One hour before end of cooking time, stir in dry macaroni.
7. Serve.

Vietnamese Beef and Noodle Soup

Prep time: 15 minutes | Cook time: 8 hours | Serves 2

- ½ pound (227 g) chuck eye roast, cut into 1-inch pieces
- 1 onion, chopped
- 3 radishes, sliced
- 3 garlic cloves, minced
- 1 serrano chile, minced
- 1 tablespoon grated fresh ginger
- 1 tablespoon freshly squeezed lime juice
- 2 teaspoons fish sauce
- 1 star anise pod
- 3 cups beef stock
- ½ teaspoon dried basil leaves
- ½ teaspoon dried marjoram leaves
- ½ teaspoon salt
- ¼ teaspoon freshly ground black pepper
- ½ (12 ounces / 340 g) package udon noodles or spaghetti
- 1 tablespoon minced fresh basil leaves
- 1 tablespoon minced fresh mint

1. Add the beef, onion, radishes, garlic, chile, ginger, lime juice, fish sauce, star anise, stock, basil, marjoram, salt, and pepper to the slow cooker and stir to combine.
2. Cover with the lid and cook on low for 7½ hours.
3. Stir in the udon noodles, cover again, and cook on high for about 20 minutes, or until the noodles are tender.
4. Mix in the fresh basil and mint, then ladle the soup into 2 bowls and serve hot.

Old-Fashioned Beef and Barley Soup

Prep time: 20 minutes | Cook time: 6 to 7 hours | Serves 8

- 2½ to 3 pounds (1.1 to 1.4 kg) beef chuck, sirloin, or flap meat, cut into ½-inch pieces
- Salt and freshly ground black pepper
- 2 tablespoons extra-virgin olive oil
- 2 cloves garlic, minced
- 2 medium onions, coarsely chopped
- 8 ounces (227 g) cremini mushrooms, quartered
- 1½ teaspoons dried thyme
- 4 medium carrots, coarsely chopped
- 3 stalks celery with leaves, coarsely chopped
- 3 tablespoons tomato paste
- 1 cup medium- to full-bodied red wine, such as Merlot, Chianti, Barolo, or Cabernet
- 6 cups beef broth
- ½ cup pearl barley

1. Season the beef evenly with 2 teaspoons salt and 1 teaspoon pepper. Heat the oil in a large skillet over high heat, then add the meat in batches, browning it on all sides. Transfer the browned beef into the insert of a 5- to 7-quart slow cooker.
2. In the same skillet over medium-high heat, sauté the garlic, onions, mushrooms, and thyme until the mushroom liquid has cooked off.
3. Pour the mixture into the slow cooker, then add the carrots and celery, stirring to combine. Deglaze the skillet with the tomato paste and wine, scraping up any browned bits, and cook until the wine reduces by about ¼ cup.
4. Add this tomato mixture to the slow-cooker insert along with the broth and barley. Cover with the lid and cook on low for 6 to 7 hours, or until the beef and barley are tender.
5. Taste and adjust the seasoning with salt and pepper before serving.

Steak Soup

Prep time: 20 minutes | Cook time: 4 to 12 hours | Serves 10 to 12

- 2 pounds (907 g) coarsely ground chuck, browned and drained
- 5 cups water
- 1 large onion, chopped
- 4 ribs celery, chopped
- 3 carrots, sliced
- 2 (14½-ounce / 411-g) cans diced tomatoes
- 1 (10-ounce / 283-g) package frozen mixed vegetables
- 5 tablespoons beef-based granules, or 5 beef bouillon cubes
- ½ teaspoon pepper
- ½ cup butter, melted
- ½ cup flour
- 2 teaspoons salt

1. Place the chuck, water, onion, celery, carrots, tomatoes, mixed vegetables, beef granules, and pepper into the slow cooker and stir to combine.
2. Cover with the lid and cook on low for 8 to 12 hours, or on high for 4 to 6 hours.
3. About an hour before serving, switch the heat to high. In a small bowl, mix the melted butter with the flour to form a smooth paste. Stir this mixture into the slow cooker until fully blended, then add salt.
4. Cover again and continue cooking on high until the mixture has thickened.

Hearty Lamb Stew

Prep time: 35 minutes | Cook time: 8 to 10 hours | Serves 6

- 2 pounds (907 g) lean lamb, cubed
- ½ teaspoon sugar
- 2 tablespoons canola oil
- 1½ teaspoons salt
- ¼ teaspoon black pepper
- ¼ cup flour
- 2 cups water
- ¾ cup red cooking wine
- ¼ teaspoon garlic powder
- 2 teaspoons Worcestershire sauce
- 6 to 8 carrots, sliced
- 4 small onions, quartered
- 4 ribs celery, sliced
- 3 medium potatoes, diced

1. Sprinkle lamb with sugar. Brown in oil in skillet.
2. Remove lamb and place in cooker, reserving drippings. Stir salt, pepper, and flour into drippings in skillet until smooth. Stir in water and wine until smooth, stirring loose the meat drippings. Continue cooking and stirring occasionally until broth simmers and thickens.
3. Pour into cooker. Add remaining ingredients and stir until well mixed.
4. Cover. Cook on low 8 to 10 hours.

Beef and Vegetable Soup

Prep time: 20 minutes | Cook time: 8 to 9 hours | Serves 8 to 10

- 1 pound (454 g) ground chuck
- 1 onion, chopped
- 2 garlic cloves, minced
- 4 cups V-8 juice
- 1 (14½-ounce / 411-g) can stewed tomatoes
- 2 cups coleslaw mix
- 2 cups frozen green beans
- 2 cups frozen corn
- 2 tablespoons Worcestershire sauce
- 1 teaspoon dried basil
- ½ teaspoon salt
- ¼ teaspoon pepper

1. Brown beef, onion, and garlic in skillet. Drain and transfer to slow cooker.
2. Add remaining ingredients to slow cooker and combine.
3. Cover. Cook on low 8 to 9 hours.

Spicy Taco Soup

Prep time: 15 minutes | Cook time: 4 to 6 hours | Serves 6 to 8

- 1 pound (454 g) ground beef
- 1 large onion, chopped
- 1 (16-ounce / 454-g) can Mexican-style tomatoes
- 1 (16-ounce / 454-g) can ranch-style beans
- 1 (16-ounce / 454-g) can whole-kernel corn, undrained
- 1 (16-ounce / 454-g) can kidney beans, undrained
- 1 (16-ounce / 454-g) can black beans, undrained
- 1 (16-ounce / 454-g) jar picante sauce
- Corn or tortilla chips
- Sour cream
- Shredded Cheddar cheese

1. Brown meat and onions in skillet. Drain.
2. Combine with all other vegetables and picante sauce in slow cooker.
3. Cover. Cook on low 4 to 6 hours.
4. Serve with corn or tortilla chips, sour cream, and shredded cheese as toppings.

Corn and Shrimp Chowder

Prep time: 20 minutes | Cook time: 3 to 4 hours | Serves 6

- 3 slices lean turkey bacon, diced
- 1 cup chopped onions
- 2 cups diced, unpeeled red potatoes
- 2 (10-ounce / 283-g) packages frozen corn
- 1 teaspoon Worcestershire sauce
- ½ teaspoon paprika
- ½ teaspoon salt
- ⅛ teaspoon black pepper
- 2 (6-ounce / 170-g) cans shrimp, drained
- 2 cups water
- 2 tablespoons butter
- 1 (12-ounce / 340-g) can fat-free evaporated milk
- Chopped chives

1. In a nonstick skillet, cook the bacon until lightly crisp. Add the onions to the drippings and sauté until translucent. Use a slotted spoon to transfer the bacon and onions to the slow cooker.
2. Add all the remaining ingredients to the cooker, reserving the milk and chives.
3. Cover and cook on low for 3 to 4 hours, then stir in the milk and chives about 30 minutes before the cooking time is finished.

Creamy Corn and Potato Chowder

Prep time: 15 minutes | Cook time: 6 hours | Serves 2

- 2 cups frozen corn kernels, thawed, divided
- ½ cup diced onion
- 1 garlic clove, minced
- 3 Yukon Gold potatoes, peeled and diced
- 2 cups low-sodium chicken broth
- 1 thyme sprig
- ⅛ teaspoon sea salt
- 2 tablespoons heavy cream (optional)
- 1 scallion, white and green parts, sliced thin, for garnish

1. Put 1½ cups of corn kernels, the onion, garlic, potatoes, broth, thyme, and salt in the slow cooker and stir together. Cover and cook on low for 6 hours.
2. Remove the thyme sprig and add the heavy cream (if using) to the crock. Purée the soup with an immersion blender until it is smooth.
3. Garnish each serving with the remaining ½ cup of corn kernels and the scallions.

Joyce's Mi

Prep time: 15 minutes | Cook time: 4 to 16 hours | Serves 6

- 3½ cups beef broth
- 1 (28-ounce / 794-g) can crushed tomatoes
- 2 medium carrots, thinly sliced
- ½ cup chopped onion
- ½ cup chopped celery
- 2 medium potatoes, thinly sliced
- 1 to 2 garlic cloves, minced
- 1 (16-ounce / 454-g) can red kidney beans, drained
- 2 ounces (57 g) thin spaghetti, broken into 2-inch pieces
- 2 tablespoons parsley flakes
- 2 to 3 teaspoons dried basil
- 1 to 2 teaspoons dried oregano
- 1 bay leaf

1. Place all the ingredients into the slow cooker and stir to combine.
2. Cover with the lid and cook on low for 10 to 16 hours, or on high for 4 to 6 hours.
3. Discard the bay leaf before serving.

Double Cheese Cauliflower Soup

Prep time: 15 minutes | Cook time: 2 to 3 hours | Serves 6

- 4 cups (1 small head) cauliflower pieces
- 2 cups water
- 1 (8-ounce / 227-g) package cream cheese, cubed
- 5 ounces (142 g) American cheese spread
- ¼ pound (113 g) dried beef, torn into strips or shredded
- ½ cup potato flakes or buds

1. In a saucepan, combine the cauliflower with water and bring to a boil. Remove from heat and set aside.
2. Turn the slow cooker to low and add the cream cheese and cheese spread. Pour in the cauliflower along with its cooking water, stirring until the cheese melts and blends with the cauliflower.
3. Stir in the dried beef and potato flakes until evenly mixed.
4. Cover the slow cooker and cook on low for 2 to 3 hours.

South Indian Classic Tomato and Pepper Soup

Prep time: 15 minutes | Cook time: 3 to 6 hours | Serves 6

- 6⅓ cups hot water
- ⅓ cup split yellow pigeon peas
- 1 tablespoon tamarind paste
- 1 heaped teaspoon black peppercorns
- 1 heaped teaspoon cumin seeds
- 1 teaspoon turmeric
- 20 curry leaves
- 6 tomatoes, roughly chopped
- 2 dried red chiles
- 4 garlic cloves, roughly chopped
- 4-inch piece fresh ginger, roughly chopped
- Handful coriander stalks, finely chopped
- Coriander leaves to garnish

1. Place all of the ingredients in the slow cooker. Cover and cook on low for 6 hours, or on high for 3 to 4 hours.
2. Use an immersion blender, or regular blender, to make a fine purée.
3. Taste and add a little more salt, if required.
4. Garnish with coriander leaves to serve.

Warming Spiced Butternut Squash Soup with Coconut Cream

Prep time: 15 minutes | Cook time: 3 to 6 hours | Serves 6

- 1 tablespoon coconut oil
- 1 teaspoon cumin seeds
- 3 garlic cloves, chopped finely
- 2 butternut squash, peeled, seeded, and chopped into chunks
- 2 red onions, peeled and chopped
- 2-inch piece fresh ginger, grated
- 2 to 3 fresh red chiles, chopped (keep some for garnish)
- 4 cups water or vegetable stock
- ⅓ cup coconut cream
- Salt to taste

1. Preheat the slow cooker on high.
2. Heat the coconut oil in a frying pan (or in the slow cooker if you have a sear setting) and add the cumin seeds. As soon as they release their aroma, add the garlic and fry for 1 minute.
3. Add the butternut squash, onions, ginger, and chiles.
4. Add the stock, cover, and cook on low for 6 hours, or on high for 3 hours.
5. Using an immersion or regular blender, purée the soup until it's smooth and thick.
6. Pour in the coconut cream and season with salt to taste. Let cook for another 10 minutes on high.
7. Check the seasoning and consistency of the soup. If it's too thick, add a little hot water.
8. Pour into bowls and top with a swirl of coconut cream and a chopped chile to garnish.

Kansas City Steak Soup

Prep time: 15 minutes | Cook time: 5 to 6 hours | Serves 6 to 8

- 2 pounds (907 g) sirloin, cut into ½-inch pieces
- 1½ teaspoons salt
- ½ teaspoon freshly ground black pepper
- 4 tablespoons (½ stick) unsalted butter
- 2 medium yellow onions, finely chopped
- 4 medium carrots, finely chopped
- 4 stalks celery with leaves, finely chopped
- 3 tablespoons all-purpose flour
- 6 cups beef broth
- 1 (16-ounce / 454-g) package frozen corn, defrosted
- 2 cups frozen petite peas, defrosted

1. Season the sirloin evenly with salt and pepper. Heat 1 tablespoon of butter in a large skillet over medium-high heat, then brown the meat in small batches on all sides. Transfer the browned pieces into the insert of a 5- to 7-quart slow cooker.
2. In the same skillet, melt the remaining 3 tablespoons of butter over medium-high heat. Add the onions, carrots, and celery, sautéing for about 5 minutes until the onions are fragrant and the vegetables begin to soften.
3. Sprinkle in the flour and cook for another 2 to 3 minutes, stirring frequently. Slowly pour in the broth, stirring until the mixture comes to a boil. Transfer everything from the skillet into the slow cooker.
4. Cover with the lid and cook on low for 4 to 5 hours, or until the sirloin is tender. Remove the lid and stir in the corn and peas.
5. Cover again and cook for an additional 45 minutes to 1 hour before serving.

Traditional Beef Stew

Prep time: 15 minutes | Cook time: 8 hours | Serves 6

- 3 tablespoons extra-virgin olive oil, divided
- 1 (2-pound / 907-g) beef chuck roast, cut into 1-inch chunks
- ½ teaspoon salt
- ¼ teaspoon freshly ground black pepper
- 2 cups beef broth
- 1 cup diced tomatoes
- ¼ cup apple cider vinegar
- 1½ cups cubed pumpkin, cut into 1-inch chunks
- ½ sweet onion, chopped
- 2 teaspoons minced garlic
- 1 teaspoon dried thyme
- 1 tablespoon chopped fresh parsley, for garnish

1. Lightly grease the insert of the slow cooker with 1 tablespoon of the olive oil.
2. Lightly season the beef chucks with salt and pepper.
3. In a large skillet over medium-high heat, heat the remaining 2 tablespoons of the olive oil. Add the beef and brown on all sides, about 7 minutes.
4. Transfer the beef to the insert and stir in the broth, tomatoes, apple cider vinegar, pumpkin, onion, garlic, and thyme.
5. Cover and cook on low heat for about 8 hours, until the beef is very tender.
6. Serve topped with the parsley.

Broccoli and Cheese Soup

Prep time: 10 minutes | Cook time: 8 to 10 hours | Serves 8

- 2 (16-ounce / 454-g) packages frozen chopped broccoli
- 2 (10¾-ounce / 305-g) cans Cheddar cheese soup
- 2 (12-ounce / 340-g) cans evaporated milk
- ¼ cup finely chopped onions
- ½ teaspoon seasoned salt
- ¼ teaspoon pepper
- Sunflower seeds (optional)
- Crumbled bacon (optional)

1. Combine all ingredients except sunflower seeds and bacon in slow cooker.
2. Cover. Cook on low 8 to 10 hours.
3. Garnish with sunflower seeds and bacon.

Sweet Potato Lentil Stew

Prep time: 15 minutes | Cook time: 5 to 6 hours | Serves 6

- 4 cups fat-free vegetable broth
- 3 cups sweet potatoes, peeled and cubed
- 1½ cups lentils, rinsed
- 3 medium carrots, cut into 1-inch pieces
- 1 medium onion, chopped
- 4 garlic cloves, minced
- ½ teaspoon ground cumin
- ¼ teaspoon ground ginger
- ¼ teaspoon cayenne pepper
- ¼ cup minced fresh cilantro or parsley
- ¼ teaspoon salt

1. Add the first nine ingredients to the slow cooker and mix well.
2. Cover and cook on low for 5 to 6 hours, or until the vegetables are just tender.
3. Stir in the cilantro and salt right before serving.

Karen's Classic Slow-Cooked Split Pea Soup

Prep time: 15 minutes | Cook time: 7 hours | Serves 6

- 2 carrots
- 2 ribs celery
- 1 onion
- 1 parsnip
- 1 leek (keep 3 inches of green)
- 1 ripe tomato
- 1 ham hock
- 1¾ cups dried split peas, washed with stones removed
- 2 tablespoons olive oil
- 1 bay leaf
- 1 teaspoon dried thyme
- 4 cups chicken broth
- 4 cups water
- 1 teaspoon salt
- ¼ teaspoon pepper
- 2 teaspoons chopped fresh parsley

1. Cut all vegetables into ¼-inch pieces and place in slow cooker. Add remaining ingredients except salt, pepper, and parsley.
2. Cover. Cook on high 7 hours.
3. Remove ham hock. Shred meat from bone and return meat to pot.
4. Season soup with salt and pepper. Stir in parsley. Serve immediately.

Sausage-Pasta Stew

Prep time: 35 minutes | Cook time: 7¼ to 9¼ hours | Serves 8

- 1 pound (454 g) Italian sausage, casings removed
- 4 cups water
- 1 (26-ounce / 737-g) jar meatless spaghetti sauce
- 1 (16-ounce / 454-g) can kidney beans, rinsed and drained
- 1 medium yellow summer squash, cut in 1-inch pieces
- 2 medium carrots, cut in ¼-inch slices
- 1 medium red or green sweet pepper, diced
- ⅓ cup chopped onions
- 1½ cups spiral pasta, uncooked
- 1 cup frozen peas
- 1 teaspoon sugar
- ½ teaspoon salt
- ¼ teaspoon pepper

1. In a skillet, sauté the sausage until it is no longer pink. Drain off any excess fat and transfer the sausage to the slow cooker.
2. Add the water, spaghetti sauce, kidney beans, squash, carrots, pepper, and onions to the cooker. Stir until everything is well combined.
3. Cover and cook on low for 7 to 9 hours, or until the vegetables are tender.
4. Stir in the remaining ingredients until evenly mixed.
5. Cover again and cook on high for 15 to 20 minutes, just until the pasta is tender.

Rutabaga and Sweet Potato Garlic Soup

Prep time: 10 minutes | Cook time: 8 hours | Serves 2

- 2 cups peeled, diced rutabaga
- 1 cup peeled, diced sweet potato
- 1 leek, white and pale green parts only, sliced thin
- ⅛ teaspoon sea salt
- 2 cups low-sodium vegetable broth
- 1 sprig fresh sage, plus 1 teaspoon minced fresh sage
- 1 teaspoon minced garlic
- 2 tablespoons toasted walnuts

1. Put the rutabaga, sweet potato, leek, salt, broth, and sprig of sage into the slow cooker.
2. Cover and cook on low for 8 hours. Remove the sage sprig.
3. Use an immersion blender to purée the soup until smooth.
4. Place the 1 teaspoon minced fresh sage, garlic, and walnuts into a mortar and pestle and grind them into a paste. Serve each bowl of soup garnished with the walnut mixture.

Turkey Minestrone

Prep time: 35 minutes | Cook time: 5 to 11 hours | Serves 10 to 12

- 3 tablespoons extra-virgin olive oil
- 1 cup chopped sweet onion
- 2 cups chopped carrots
- 2 cups chopped celery
- 2 teaspoons chopped fresh rosemary
- ½ cup dry white wine
- 1 (14- to 15-ounce / 397- to 425-g) can chopped tomatoes, with their juice
- 5 cups chicken broth
- Rind from Parmigiano-Reggiano cheese, cut into ½-inch pieces (optional)
- 3 medium zucchini, diced (about 1½ cups)
- 1 cup 1-inch pieces green beans
- 4 cups bite-size pieces cooked turkey or chicken
- 1 (15-ounce / 425-g) can small white beans or garbanzo beans, drained and rinsed
- 1 head escarole, tough leaves removed, cut into 1-inch pieces, or 2 (10-ounce / 283-g) bags baby spinach
- 1 teaspoon salt (you will need more if you don't use the cheese rind)
- 1 teaspoon freshly ground black pepper
- 12 ounces (340 g) fresh cheese tortellini, cooked according to package directions and drained
- 1 cup freshly grated Parmigiano-Reggiano cheese, for garnish

1. In a large skillet, heat the oil over medium-high heat.
2. Add the onion, carrots, celery, and rosemary, cooking for about 6 minutes until the vegetables start to soften. Stir in the wine, let it boil for 2 minutes, and then add the tomatoes. Continue cooking for 4 minutes so that some of the liquid cooks off.
3. Move the mixture from the skillet into the insert of a 5- to 7-quart slow cooker. Pour in the broth and drop in the cheese rind if using. Add the zucchini, green beans, turkey, white beans, and escarole, stirring everything together.
4. Put the lid on and cook for 4 hours on high, or 8 to 10 hours on low.
5. When ready, adjust the flavour with salt and pepper. Stir the cooked tortellini into the soup, then cover once more and cook for an additional 30 minutes on high or 1 hour on low.
6. Finish by sprinkling Parmigiano-Reggiano cheese on top just before serving.

Mediterranean Vegetable Stew

Prep time: 25 minutes | Cook time: 8 to 10 hours | Serves 10

- 1 butternut squash, peeled, seeded, and cubed
- 2 cups unpeeled cubed eggplant
- 2 cups cubed zucchini
- 10 ounces (283 g) fresh okra, cut into slices
- 1 (8-ounce / 227-g) can tomato sauce
- 1 large yellow onion, chopped
- 1 ripe tomato, chopped
- 1 carrot, thinly sliced
- ½ cup vegetable stock
- ⅓ cup raisins
- 2 cloves garlic, minced
- ½ teaspoon ground cumin
- ½ teaspoon ground turmeric
- ¼ teaspoon red pepper flakes
- ¼ teaspoon ground cinnamon
- 1 teaspoon paprika

1. Place the butternut squash, eggplant, zucchini, okra, tomato sauce, onion, tomato, carrot, vegetable stock, raisins, and garlic into the slow cooker. Add the cumin, turmeric, red pepper flakes, cinnamon, and paprika, sprinkling them evenly over the top.
2. Cover with the lid and cook on low for 8 to 10 hours, until the vegetables are soft enough to pierce easily with a fork. Serve hot.

Rich Vegetable Stock

Prep time: 20 minutes | Cook time: 5 to 10 hours | Makes about 8 cups

- ¼ cup olive oil
- 2 large sweet onions, such as Vidalia, coarsely chopped
- 4 large carrots, cut into 1-inch chunks
- 4 stalks celery with leaves, cut into 2-inch pieces
- 4 medium parsnips, cut into 1-inch chunks
- 8 ounces (227 g) cremini mushrooms, quartered
- 2 tablespoons tomato paste
- 1 bunch Swiss chard, cut into 1-inch pieces (about 3 cups)
- 2 teaspoons dried thyme
- 1 bay leaf
- 2 teaspoons salt
- ½ teaspoon whole black peppercorns
- 2 cups water

1. Put all the ingredients into the insert of a 5- to 7-quart slow cooker and toss to combine. Cover and cook on high for 5 hours or on low for 8 to 10 hours.
2. Remove the cover and take out the large pieces of vegetables with a slotted spoon. Strain the stock through a fine-mesh sieve and discard the solids.
3. Skim off any fat from the top of the stock. Refrigerate for up to 5 days or freeze for up to 6 months.

Quick Beef Stew

Prep time: 20 minutes | Cook time: 7½ to 8½ hours | Serves 4 to 6

4 medium red potatoes

1½ pounds (680 g) beef stew meat

⅓ cup flour

1 (14-ounce / 397-g) diced tomatoes, undrained

2 cups water

3 cups frozen stir-fry bell peppers and onions

1. Cut potatoes into quarters. Place on bottom of slow cooker.
2. In a mixing bowl, toss flour with beef to coat. Add to slow cooker.
3. Pour in undrained tomatoes and water.
4. Cover and cook on low 7 to 8 hours, or until beef and potatoes are tender but not overcooked.
5. Gently fold stir-fry vegetables into stew. Cover and cook on low 30 to 40 minutes, or until vegetables are hot and tender.

Crab Meat Soup

Prep time: 10 minutes | Cook time: 5 to 6 hours | Serves 8

- 2 (10¾-ounce / 305-g) cans cream of tomato soup
- 2 (10½-ounce / 298-g) cans split pea soup
- 3 cans milk
- 1 cup heavy cream
- 1 or 2 (6-ounce / 170-g) cans crab meat, drained
- ¼ cup sherry (optional)

1. Into the slow cooker, pour the soups, then add the milk and stir well to blend.
2. Place the lid on and cook on low for about 4 hours, or until the mixture is piping hot.
3. Mix in the cream and crab meat, re-cover, and let cook on low for another hour, just until fully warmed through.

German Potato Soup

Prep time: 15 minutes | Cook time: 4 to 10 hours | Serves 6 to 8

- 1 onion, chopped
- 1 leek, trimmed and diced
- 2 carrots, diced
- 1 cup chopped cabbage
- ¼ cup chopped fresh parsley
- 4 cups beef broth
- 1 pound (454 g) potatoes, diced
- 1 bay leaf
- 1 to 2 teaspoons black pepper
- 1 teaspoon salt (optional)
- ½ teaspoon caraway seeds (optional)
- ¼ teaspoon nutmeg
- 1 pound (454 g) bacon, cooked and crumbled
- ½ cup sour cream

1. Place all the ingredients in the slow cooker, except for the bacon and sour cream.
2. Cover and cook on low for 8 to 10 hours, or on high for 4 to 5 hours.
3. Remove the bay leaf. With a slotted spoon, take out the potatoes, mash them, and blend with the sour cream. Return this mixture to the slow cooker, stir well, then add the bacon and mix until combined.

Low-Calorie Soup

Prep time: 15 minutes | Cook time: 5 hours | Serves 14

- 2 cups thinly sliced celery
- 2 cups chopped cabbage
- 1 (8-ounce / 227-g) package frozen green beans
- 1 onion, chopped
- 1 (28-ounce / 794-g) can diced tomatoes
- 3 envelopes dry low-sodium beef-flavoured soup mix
- 3 tablespoons Worcestershire sauce
- ½ teaspoon salt
- ¼ teaspoon black pepper
- Water to cover

1. Place all the ingredients into the slow cooker and stir to mix them together.
2. Cover with the lid and cook on high for 5 hours.

Chapter 8

Snacks and Appetizers

Chapter 8 Snacks and Appetizers

Butterscotch Haystacks

Prep time: 15 minutes | Cook time: 15 minutes | Makes 3 dozen pieces

- 2 (6-ounce / 170-g) packages butterscotch chips
- ¾ cup chopped almonds
- 1 (5-ounce / 142-g) can chow mein noodles

1. Switch the cooker to high and add the chips to the insert. Stir every few minutes until the chips are fully melted.
2. Once melted, gently fold in the almonds and noodles until evenly coated.
3. Drop the mixture by teaspoonfuls onto sheets of waxed paper.
4. Allow the haystacks to set at room temperature, or refrigerate to speed up the process.
5. Serve once firm, or store in a covered container with waxed paper between the layers. Keep in a cool, dry place.

Reuben Spread

Prep time: 10 minutes | Cook time: 4 hours | Serves 3

- 2 (8-ounce / 227-g) packages cream cheese, cubed
- 4 cups shredded Swiss cheese
- 1 (14-ounce / 397-g) can sauerkraut, rinsed and well drained
- 4 (2-ounce / 57-g) packages thinly sliced deli corned beef, chopped
- ½ cup Thousand Island salad dressing
- Snack rye bread or rye crackers

1. Add the first five ingredients to a 1½-quart slow cooker and stir until well combined. Cover and cook on low for 4 to 4½ hours, or until thoroughly heated.
2. Stir again to blend before serving. Spread on bread to enjoy.

Snack Mix

Prep time: 10 minutes | Cook time: 2 hours | Serves 10 to 14

- 8 cups Chex cereal, of any combination
- 6 cups pretzels
- 6 tablespoons butter, melted
- 2 tablespoons Worcestershire sauce
- 1 teaspoon seasoned salt
- ½ teaspoon garlic powder
- ½ teaspoon onion salt
- ½ teaspoon onion powder

1. Place the first two ingredients into the slow cooker.
2. Mix the butter with the seasonings, then pour it over the dry ingredients. Toss until everything is evenly coated.
3. Cover with the lid and cook on low for 2 hours, stirring every 30 minutes.

Chocolate Peanut Clusters

Prep time: 20 minutes | Cook time: 3 hours | Makes 3½ to 4 dozen pieces

- 2 pounds (907 g) white candy coating, chopped
- 1 (12-ounce / 340-g) package semi-sweet chocolate chips
- 1 (4-ounce / 113-g) milk chocolate bar, or 1 (4-ounce / 113-g) package German sweet chocolate, chopped
- 1 (24-ounce / 680-g) jar dry roasted peanuts
- Nonstick cooking spray

1. Spray inside of slow cooker with nonstick cooking spray.
2. In slow cooker, combine white candy coating, chocolate chips, and milk chocolate.
3. Cover and cook on low 3 hours. Stir every 15 minutes.
4. Add peanuts to melted chocolate. Mix well.
5. Drop by tablespoonfuls onto waxed paper. Cool until set. Serve immediately, or store in a tightly covered container, separating layers with waxed paper. Keep cool and dry.

Kielbasa with Apples

Prep time: 15 minutes | Cook time: 6 to 8 hours | Serves 12

- 2 pounds (907 g) fully cooked kielbasa sausage, cut into 1-inch pieces
- ¾ cup brown sugar
- 1 cup chunky applesauce
- 2 cloves garlic, minced

1. Combine all ingredients in slow cooker.
2. Cover and cook on low 6 to 8 hours until thoroughly heated.

Kielbasa in Spicy Barbecue Sauce

Prep time: 20 minutes | Cook time: 4 to 5 hours | Serves 8

- 2 cups ketchup
- ½ cup firmly packed light brown sugar
- 1 tablespoon Worcestershire sauce
- 1 teaspoon Creole mustard
- 1 teaspoon hot sauce
- 1 medium onion, finely chopped
- ½ cup bourbon
- 2 pounds (907 g) kielbasa or other smoked sausages, cut into ½-inch rounds

1. Place all the ingredients into the insert of a 3- to 5-quart slow cooker. Cover with the lid and cook on low for 4 to 5 hours, until the sausage is fully heated.
2. Keep the kielbasa warm in the cooker and serve with 6-inch skewers.

Butter-Curried Crispy Almonds

Prep time: 5 minutes | Cook time: 3 to 4½ hours | Makes 4 cups nuts

- 2 tablespoons butter, melted
- 1 tablespoon curry powder
- ½ teaspoon seasoned salt
- 1 pound (454 g) blanched almonds

1. Combine butter with curry powder and seasoned salt.
2. Pour over almonds in slow cooker. Mix to coat well.
3. Cover. Cook on low 2 to 3 hours. Turn to high. Uncover cooker and cook 1 to 1½ hours.
4. Serve hot or cold.

Bacon-Pineapple Tater Tot Bake

Prep time: 15 minutes | Cook time: 4 hours | Serves 8

- 1 (32-ounce / 907-g) package frozen tater tots, thawed
- 8 ounces (227 g) Canadian bacon, chopped
- 1 cup frozen pepper strips, thawed and chopped
- 1 medium onion, finely chopped
- 1 (8-ounce / 227-g) can pineapple tidbits, drained
- 2 eggs
- 3 (5-ounce / 142-g) cans evaporated milk
- 1 (15-ounce / 425-g) can pizza sauce
- 1 cup shredded provolone cheese
- ½ cup grated Parmesan cheese (optional)

1. Grease a 5-quart slow cooker and spread half of the Tater Tots on the bottom. Add layers of Canadian bacon, peppers, onion, and pineapple, then cover with the remaining Tater Tots. In a large bowl, whisk together the eggs, milk, and pizza sauce, then pour the mixture over the layers. Sprinkle provolone cheese evenly on top.
2. Cover and cook on low for 4 to 5 hours, or until fully heated. If you like, sprinkle with Parmesan cheese, then let stand covered for 20 minutes before serving.

Sweet and Sour Meatballs

Prep time: 10 minutes | Cook time: 2 to 4 hours | Serves 15 to 20

- 1 (12-ounce / 340-g) jar grape jelly
- 1 (12-ounce / 340-g) jar chili sauce
- 2 (1-pound / 454-g) bags prepared frozen meatballs, thawed

1. Combine jelly and sauce in slow cooker. Stir well.
2. Add meatballs. Stir to coat.
3. Cover and heat on low 4 hours, or on high 2 hours. Keep slow cooker on low while serving.

Everyone's favourite Snack Mix

Prep time: 20 minutes | Cook time: 2 hours | Serves 8 to 10

- ½ cup (2 sticks) unsalted butter, melted
- 2 tablespoons Lawry's seasoned salt
- 1 tablespoon garlic salt
- ¼ cup Worcestershire sauce
- 6 shakes Tabasco sauce
- 4 cups Crispix cereal
- 2 cups mixed nuts
- 1 (8- to 10-ounce / 227- to 283-g) bag pretzel sticks
- 1 (5-ounce / 142-g) bag plain or Parmesan goldfish crackers
- 2 (3-ounce / 85-g) bags herbed croutons

1. In the insert of a 5- to 7-quart slow cooker, mix together the butter, seasoned salt, garlic salt, Worcestershire, and Tabasco until blended. Add the remaining ingredients and stir gently so everything is evenly coated in the butter mixture.
2. Cook uncovered on high for 2 hours, stirring now and then. Lower the heat to low and continue cooking for 1 more hour, stirring every 15 minutes, until the mix becomes dry and crisp.
3. Spread the mixture onto baking sheets to cool completely, then serve, or store in airtight containers.

Spicy Rasta Wings

Prep time: 15 minutes | Cook time: 3 hours | Serves 8

- 3 pounds (1.4 kg) chicken wing drumettes
- 2 teaspoons jerk seasoning
- 1½ cups mango nectar
- ¼ cup firmly packed light brown sugar

1. Lightly spray the insert of a 5- to 7-quart slow cooker with nonstick cooking spray.
2. Place the wings on a rack set over a baking sheet and broil until they crisp on one side.
3. Flip the wings and broil the other side for about 5 minutes, until browned and crispy.
4. Remove the wings from the oven. For advance prep, let them cool and refrigerate for up to 2 days; otherwise, transfer them straight into the prepared slow-cooker insert.
5. In a mixing bowl, combine the remaining ingredients, then pour the sauce over the wings and turn them until well coated.
6. Cover with the lid and cook on high for 3 hours, turning the wings twice during cooking.
7. Serve the wings directly from the slow cooker on the warm setting.

Artichoke Party Bites

Prep time: 10 minutes | Cook time: 2½ to 4 hours | Serves 4

- 4 whole, fresh artichokes
- 1 teaspoon salt
- 4 tablespoons lemon juice, divided
- 2 tablespoons butter, melted

1. Wash and trim off the tough outer leaves and around the bottom of the artichokes. Cut off about 1 inch from the tops of each, and trim off the tips of the leaves. Spread the top leaves apart and use a long-handled spoon to pull out the fuzzy chokes in their centers.
2. Stand the prepared artichokes upright in the slow cooker. Sprinkle each with ¼ teaspoon salt.
3. Spoon 2 tablespoons lemon juice over the artichokes. Pour in enough water to cover the bottom half of the artichokes.
4. Cover and cook on high for 2½ to 4 hours.
5. Serve with melted butter and remaining lemon juice for dipping.

Hot Crab Dip

Prep time: 20 minutes | Cook time: 1½ hours | Makes 2⅓ cups

- 1 (8-ounce / 227-g) package cream cheese, softened
- 2 green onions, chopped
- ¼ cup chopped sweet red pepper
- 2 tablespoons minced fresh parsley
- 2 tablespoons mayonnaise
- 1 tablespoon Dijon mustard
- 1 teaspoon Worcestershire sauce
- ¼ teaspoon salt
- ¼ teaspoon pepper
- 2 (6-ounce / 170-g) cans lump crabmeat, drained
- 2 tablespoons capers, drained
- Dash hot pepper sauce
- Assorted crackers

1. In a 1½-quart slow cooker, combine the first nine ingredients; stir in crab.
2. Cover and cook on low for 1 to 2 hours. Stir in capers and pepper sauce; cook 30 minutes longer to allow flavours to blend. Serve with crackers.

Rich Honey-Glazed Smoked Little Sausages in Barbecue Sauce

Prep time: 15 minutes | Cook time: 2 to 3 hours | Serves 6 to 8

- 2 (16-ounce / 454-g) packages mini smoked sausages (Hillshire Farms is a reliable brand)
- 2 tablespoons canola or vegetable oil
- 1 medium onion, finely chopped
- 2 teaspoons ancho chile powder
- 1½ cups ketchup
- 1 (8-ounce / 227-g) can tomato sauce
- ¼ cup molasses
- 2 tablespoons Worcestershire sauce
- ¼ cup honey

1. Arrange the sausages in the insert of a 1½- to 3-quart slow cooker. Heat the oil in a small skillet over medium-high heat. Add the onion and chili powder and sauté until the onion is softened, about 3 minutes.
2. Transfer the contents of the skillet to the slow-cooker insert. Add the ketchup, tomato sauce, molasses, Worcestershire, and honey and stir to blend. Cover and cook over low heat 2 to 3 hours, until the sausages are heated through.
3. Serve the sausages from the cooker set on warm.

Roasted Tomato and Mozzarella Bruschetta

Prep time: 15 minutes | Cook time: 5 hours | Serves 8

- ¼ cup extra-virgin olive oil
- 1 large red onion, coarsely chopped
- 2 teaspoons dried basil
- 1 teaspoon fresh rosemary leaves, finely chopped
- 4 cloves garlic, minced
- 3 (28- to 32-ounce / 794- to 907-g) cans whole plum tomatoes, drained
- 2 teaspoons salt
- ⅛ teaspoon red pepper flakes
- 8 ounces (227 g) fresh Mozzarella, cut into ½-inch dice

1. Prepare lightly toasted baguette slices to serve alongside.
2. In the insert of a 5- to 7-quart slow cooker, combine all ingredients except the Mozzarella and baguette. Cover and cook on high for 2 hours. Uncover and continue cooking on low for about 3 hours, stirring occasionally, until most of the tomato liquid has cooked off.
3. Transfer the tomato mixture to a food processor and pulse about five times to chop the tomatoes and garlic. Move to a serving bowl to cool slightly, then stir in the Mozzarella.
4. Serve the mixture with the toasted baguette slices.

Buffet Meat favourites

Prep time: 5 minutes | Cook time: 2 hours | Serves 24

- 1 cup tomato sauce
- 1 teaspoon Worcestershire sauce
- ½ teaspoon prepared mustard
- 2 tablespoons brown sugar
- 1 pound (454 g) prepared meatballs or mini-wieners

1. Mix first four ingredients in slow cooker.
2. Add meatballs or mini-wieners.
3. Cover and cook on high for 2 hours. Turn to low and serve as an appetizer from the slow cooker.

Warm Clam Dip

Prep time: 15 minutes | Cook time: 2 to 3 hours | Serves 6 to 8

- 2 (8-ounce / 227-g) packages cream cheese at room temperature and cut into cubes
- ½ cup mayonnaise
- 3 green onions, finely chopped, using the white and tender green parts
- 2 cloves garlic, minced
- 3 (8-ounce / 227-g) cans minced or chopped clams, drained with ¼ cup clam juice reserved
- 1 tablespoon Worcestershire sauce
- 2 teaspoons anchovy paste
- ¼ cup finely chopped fresh Italian parsley

1. Lightly coat the insert of a 1½- to 3-quart slow cooker with nonstick cooking spray. In a large mixing bowl, combine all the ingredients, using the clam juice to thin the dip as needed.
2. Pour the mixture into the prepared slow cooker, cover, and cook on low for 2 to 3 hours, until hot and bubbling.
3. Serve directly from the cooker on the warm setting.

Barbecued Party Starters

Prep time: 30 minutes | Cook time: 2¼ hours | Serves 16

- 1 pound (454 g) ground beef
- ¼ cup finely chopped onion
- 1 (16-ounce / 454-g) package miniature hot dogs, drained
- 1 (12-ounce / 340-g) jar apricot preserves
- 1 cup barbecue sauce
- 1 (20-ounce / 567-g) can pineapple chunks, drained

1. Mix the beef and onion together gently but thoroughly in a large bowl, then shape into 1-inch meatballs. Cook the meatballs in a large skillet over medium heat in two batches, turning occasionally, until fully cooked.
2. With a slotted spoon, transfer the meatballs to a 3-quart slow cooker. Add the hot dogs, then stir in the preserves and barbecue sauce. Cover and cook on high for 2 to 3 hours, until everything is heated through.
3. Stir in the pineapple, cover again, and cook for an additional 15 to 20 minutes, just until the mixture is hot.

Hot Bloody Mary Dip for Shrimp

Prep time: 15 minutes | Cook time: 3 to 4 hours | Serves 8

- 2 (8-ounce / 227-g) packages cream cheese at room temperature, cut into cubes
- 1½ cups Clamato juice
- 2 cups spicy tomato juice or bloody Mary mix
- 2 tablespoons prepared horseradish
- ⅓ cup Worcestershire sauce
- 1 teaspoon Tabasco sauce
- 2 teaspoons celery salt
- ¼ teaspoon freshly ground black pepper
- 2 tablespoons fresh lemon juice
- 1 cup pepper vodka
- 4 green onions, finely chopped, using the white and tender green parts
- 4 stalks celery, finely chopped

1. Spray the insert of a 3- to 5-quart slow cooker with nonstick cooking spray. Place the cream cheese inside, cover, and let it cook on low for 20 minutes until softened. Add the rest of the ingredients and stir until combined.
2. Cover again and cook on low for 3 to 4 hours, stirring occasionally during the cooking process.
3. Keep the cooker on warm and serve directly from it.

Artichoke Dip with Cream

Prep time: 20 minutes | Cook time: 1 hour | Makes 5 cups

- 2 (14-ounce / 397-g) cans water-packed artichoke hearts, rinsed, drained and coarsely chopped
- 2 cups shredded part-skim mozzarella cheese
- 1 (8-ounce / 227-g) package cream cheese, cubed
- 1 cup shredded Parmesan cheese
- ½ cup mayonnaise
- ½ cup shredded Swiss cheese
- 2 tablespoons lemon juice
- 2 tablespoons plain yoghurt
- 1 tablespoon seasoned salt
- 1 tablespoon chopped seeded jalapeno pepper
- 1 teaspoon garlic powder
- Tortilla chips

1. In a 3-quart slow cooker, combine the first 11 ingredients. Cover and cook on low for 1 hour or until heated through. Serve with tortilla chips.

Pickled Whiting Fish

Prep time: 10 minutes | Cook time: 3 to 4 hours | Serves 24

- 2 onions, sliced
- 1 cup white vinegar
- ¾ cup Splenda
- 1 teaspoon salt
- 1 tablespoon allspice
- 2 pounds (907 g) frozen individual whiting with skin

1. Combine onions, vinegar, Splenda, salt, and allspice in bottom of slow cooker.
2. Slice frozen whiting into 2-inch slices, each with skin on. Place fish in slow cooker, pushing it down into the liquid as much as possible.
3. Cook on low 3 to 4 hours.
4. Pour cooking liquid over fish, cover, and refrigerate. Serve when well chilled.

Garlic Swiss Fondue

Prep time: 10 minutes | Cook time: 2 hours | Makes 3 cups

- 4 cups shredded Swiss cheese
- 1 (10¾-ounce / 305-g) can condensed cheddar cheese soup, undiluted
- 2 tablespoons sherry or chicken broth
- 1 tablespoon Dijon mustard
- 2 garlic cloves, minced
- 2 teaspoons hot pepper sauce
- Cubed French bread baguette
- Sliced apples
- Seedless red grapes

1. In a 1½-quart slow cooker, combine the first six ingredients. Cover and cook on low for 2 to 2½ hours, stirring every 30 minutes, until the cheese is fully melted. Serve warm with bread cubes and fruit.

Spicy Jalapeno Spinach Dip

Prep time: 10 minutes | Cook time: 2 hours | Serves 6

- 2 (10-ounce / 283-g) packages frozen chopped spinach, thawed and squeezed dry
- 2 (8-ounce / 227-g) packages cream cheese, softened
- 1 cup grated Parmesan cheese
- 1 cup half-and-half cream
- ½ cup finely chopped onion
- ¼ cup chopped seeded jalapeno peppers
- 2 teaspoons Worcestershire sauce
- 2 teaspoons hot pepper sauce
- 1 teaspoon garlic powder
- 1 teaspoon dill weed
- Tortilla chips

1. In a small bowl, combine the cream cheese, dressing, sour cream and blue cheese. Transfer to a 3-quart slow cooker. Layer with chicken, wing sauce and 1 cup cheese. Cover and cook on low for 2 to 3 hours or until heated through.
2. Sprinkle with remaining cheese and onion. Serve with tortilla chips.

Southwestern Queso Dip

Prep time: 20 minutes | Cook time: 2 to 3 hours | Serves 8

- 1 (8-ounce / 227-g) package cream cheese, cut into cubes
- 2 tablespoons unsalted butter
- 1 medium sweet onion, such as Vidalia, finely chopped
- 4 chipotle chiles in adobo, minced
- 1 medium red bell pepper, seeded and finely chopped
- 1 medium yellow bell pepper, seeded and finely chopped
- 2 teaspoons ground cumin
- 2 cups finely shredded sharp Cheddar cheese
- 2 cups finely shredded Monterey Jack cheese
- Fresh vegetables for serving
- Tortilla chips for serving

1. Coat the insert of a 1½- to 3-quart slow cooker with nonstick cooking spray. Turn the machine on low and add the cream cheese. Cover and let stand while preparing the other ingredients.
2. Melt the butter in a large sauté pan over medium-high heat. Add the onion, chipotles, bell peppers, and cumin and sauté until the bell peppers become softened, 4 to 5 minutes. Transfer the contents of the sauté pan into the slow-cooker insert and stir to blend with the cream cheese.
3. Fold in the Cheddar and Jack cheeses. Cover and cook on low for 2 to 3 hours.
4. Serve from the cooker set on warm with fresh vegetables and sturdy tortilla chips.

Chapter 9

Vegetables and Sides

Chapter 9 Vegetables and Sides

Creamy Broccoli Casserole

Prep time: 15 minutes | Cook time: 6 hours | Serves 6

- 1 tablespoon extra-virgin olive oil
- 1 pound (454 g) broccoli, cut into florets
- 1 pound (454 g) cauliflower, cut into florets
- ¼ cup almond flour
- 2 cups coconut milk
- ½ teaspoon ground nutmeg
- Pinch freshly ground black pepper
- 1½ cups shredded Gouda cheese, divided

1. Lightly coat the insert of the slow cooker with olive oil.
2. Add the broccoli and cauliflower to the cooker.
3. In a small bowl, mix together the almond flour, coconut milk, nutmeg, pepper, and 1 cup of cheese.
4. Pour this mixture over the vegetables, then sprinkle the remaining ½ cup of cheese on top.
5. Cover with the lid and cook on low for 6 hours.
6. Serve the casserole warm.

Mashed Sweet Potatoes with Garlic

Prep time: 20 minutes | Cook time: 8 hours | Serves 1 cup

- Nonstick cooking spray
- 4 large sweet potatoes, peeled and cubed
- 1 onion, chopped
- 6 garlic cloves, peeled
- ½ cup orange juice
- 2 tablespoons honey
- 1 teaspoon salt
- ⅛ teaspoon freshly ground black pepper
- ⅓ cup butter, at room temperature
- ½ cup heavy cream

1. Coat the inside of the slow cooker with nonstick cooking spray.
2. Add the sweet potatoes, onion, and garlic directly into the cooker.
3. Pour in the orange juice and honey, stir to combine, then season with salt and pepper.
4. Cover and cook on low for 8 hours, or until the sweet potatoes are very tender.
5. Stir in the butter and cream, mash with a potato masher or blend with an immersion blender, and serve warm.

Garlic Potatoes

Prep time: 10 minutes | Cook time: 5 to 6 hours | Serves 6

- 6 potatoes, peeled and cubed
- 6 garlic cloves, minced
- ¼ cup dried onion, or 1 medium onion, chopped
- 2 tablespoons olive oil

1. Combine all ingredients in slow cooker.
2. Cook on low 5 to 6 hours, or until potatoes are soft but not turning brown.

Sweet Potato Dressing

Prep time: 15 minutes | Cook time: 4 hours | Serves 8

- ½ cup chopped celery
- ½ cup chopped onions
- ¼ cup butter
- 6 cups dry bread cubes
- 1 large sweet potato, cooked, peeled, and cubed
- ½ cup chicken broth
- ¼ cup chopped pecans
- ½ teaspoon poultry seasoning
- ½ teaspoon rubbed sage
- ½ teaspoon salt
- ¼ teaspoon pepper

1. Sauté celery and onion in skillet in butter until tender. Pour into greased slow cooker.
2. Add remaining ingredients. Toss gently.
3. Cover. Cook on low 4 hours.

Carrots with Orange Thyme Glaze

Prep time: 10 minutes | Cook time: 4 to 6 hours | Serves 6 to 8

- ½ cup (1 stick) unsalted butter, melted
- ¼ cup honey
- 1 cup orange juice
- Grated zest of 1 orange
- 1 teaspoon dried thyme
- ½ cup chicken broth
- 2 (16-ounce / 454-g) bags baby carrots

1. Coat the insert of a 5- to 7-quart slow cooker with nonstick cooking spray or line it with a slow-cooker liner according to the manufacturer's directions.
2. Combine all the ingredients in the slow cooker and stir to coat the carrots. Cover and cook on low for 4 to 6 hours, until the carrots are tender.
3. Serve the carrots from the cooker set on warm.

Apple-flavoured Stuffing

Prep time: 20 minutes | Cook time: 4 to 5 hours | Serves 4 to 5

- 1 stick (½ cup) butter, divided
- 1 cup chopped walnuts
- 2 onions, chopped
- 1 (14-ounce / 397-g) package dry herb-seasoned stuffing mix
- 1½ cups applesauce
- Water (optional)
- Nonstick cooking spray

1. In nonstick skillet, melt 2 tablespoons of butter. Sauté walnuts over medium heat until toasted, about 5 minutes, stirring frequently. Remove from skillet and set aside.
2. Melt remaining butter in skillet. Add onions and cook 3 to 4 minutes, or until almost tender. Set aside.
3. Spray slow cooker with nonstick cooking spray. Place dry stuffing mix in slow cooker.
4. Add onion-butter mixture and stir. Add applesauce and stir.
5. Cover and cook on low 4 to 5 hours, or until heated through. Check after Stuffing has cooked for 3½ hours. If it's sticking to the cooker, drying out, or becoming too brown on the edges, stir in ½ to 1 cup water. Continue cooking.
6. Sprinkle with walnuts before serving.

Cheesy Hash Browns

Prep time: 10 minutes | Cook time: 7 hours | Serves ¾ cup

- Nonstick cooking spray
- 1 (20 ounces / 567 g) package frozen hash brown potatoes
- 1 onion, finely chopped
- 3 garlic cloves, minced
- 1 cup grated Colby or Gruyère cheese
- 1 cup milk
- ⅓ cup heavy cream
- 3 tablespoons butter
- ½ teaspoon dried marjoram leaves
- ¼ teaspoon salt
- ⅛ teaspoon freshly ground black pepper
- ½ cup sour cream

1. Lightly spray the inside of the slow cooker with nonstick cooking spray.
2. Place the hash brown potatoes, onion, and garlic in the cooker, give them a stir, and fold in the cheese.
3. In a small saucepan set over high heat, combine the milk, cream, butter, marjoram, salt, and pepper. Let the mixture heat just until the butter has melted, about 1 minute, then take it off the heat and whisk in the sour cream.
4. Pour this hot milk mixture over the contents of the slow cooker, stirring gently to combine.
5. Cover and cook on low for 7 hours, or until the potatoes are fork-tender. Serve straight from the cooker while hot.

Potatoes with Mustard

Prep time: 5 minutes | Cook time: 2 to 4 hours | Serves 6

- ½ cup onions, chopped
- 1 tablespoon butter
- 1½ teaspoons prepared mustard
- 1 teaspoon salt
- ¼ teaspoon black pepper
- ½ cup fat-free or 2% milk
- ¼ pound (113 g) low-fat cheese, shredded
- 6 medium potatoes, cooked and grated

1. Sauté onion in butter in skillet. Add mustard, salt, pepper, milk, and cheese.
2. Place potatoes in slow cooker. Do not press down.
3. Pour mixture over potatoes.
4. Cover. Cook on low 3 to 4 hours.
5. Toss potatoes with a large spoon when ready to serve.

Glazed Golden Carrots

Prep time: 5 minutes | Cook time: 3 to 4 hours | Serves 6

- 1 (2-pound / 907-g) package baby carrots
- ½ cup golden raisins
- 1 stick butter, melted or softened
- ⅓ cup honey
- 2 tablespoons lemon juice
- ½ teaspoon ground ginger (optional)

1. Combine all ingredients in slow cooker.
2. Cover and cook on low 3 to 4 hours, or until carrots are tender-crisp.

Savoury Butternut Squash and Apples

Prep time: 10 minutes | Cook time: 4 hours | Serves 10

- 1 (3-pound / 1.4-kg) butternut squash, peeled, seeded, and cubed
- 4 cooking apples (Granny Smith or Honeycrisp), peeled, cored, and chopped
- ¾ cup dried currants
- ½ sweet yellow onion such as Vidalia, sliced thin
- 1 tablespoon ground cinnamon
- 1½ teaspoons ground nutmeg

1. Place the squash, apples, currants, and onion into the slow cooker, then sprinkle the mixture with cinnamon and nutmeg.
2. Cover and cook on high for 4 hours, stirring now and then, until the squash is tender and fully cooked.

Potatoes Baked in the Crock

Prep time: 10 minutes | Cook time: 3 to 8 hours | Serves 8 to 10

- 8 russet baking potatoes, scrubbed
- ½ cup extra-virgin olive oil
- 1 tablespoon salt
- 1 teaspoon coarsely ground black pepper

1. Use the tip of a sharp knife to prick each potato several times. In a bowl, mix together the oil, salt, and pepper, then rub the mixture evenly over the potatoes.
2. Place the seasoned potatoes into the insert of a 5- to 7-quart slow cooker. Cover with the lid and cook on high for 3 to 4 hours, or on low for 7 to 8 hours.
3. Take the potatoes out of the slow cooker to serve, or keep them in the cooker on warm for serving.

Green Beans Greek Style

Prep time: 5 minutes | Cook time: 2 to 5 hours | Serves 6

- 20 ounces (567 g) whole or cut-up frozen green beans (not French cut)
- 2 cups tomato sauce
- 2 teaspoons dried onion flakes (optional)
- Pinch of dried marjoram or oregano
- Pinch of ground nutmeg
- Pinch of cinnamon

1. Combine all ingredients in slow cooker, mixing together thoroughly.
2. Cover and cook on low 2 to 4 hours if the beans are defrosted, or 3 to 5 hours on low if the beans are frozen, or until the beans are done to your liking.

Quick Broccoli Fix

Prep time: 15 minutes | Cook time: 5 to 6 hours | Serves 6

- 1 pound (454 g) fresh or frozen broccoli, cut up
- 1 (10¾-ounce / 305-g) can cream of mushroom soup
- ½ cup mayonnaise
- ½ cup plain yoghurt
- ½ pound (227 g) sliced fresh mushrooms
- 1 cup shredded Cheddar cheese, divided
- 1 cup crushed saltine crackers
- Sliced almonds (optional)

1. Microwave the broccoli for 3 minutes, then transfer it to a greased slow cooker.
2. In a bowl, mix together the soup, mayonnaise, yoghurt, mushrooms, and ½ cup of cheese. Pour this mixture over the broccoli.
3. Cover with the lid and cook on low for 5 to 6 hours.
4. During the last 30 minutes of cooking, sprinkle the remaining cheese and add the crackers on top.
5. For a finishing touch, top with sliced almonds just before serving.

Tomato, Corn, and Yellow Squash with Dill Butter

Prep time: 10 minutes | Cook time: 1½ to 2 hours | Serves 6 to 8

- ½ cup (1 stick) unsalted butter, melted
- 1 teaspoon salt
- ½ teaspoon freshly ground black pepper
- 2 tablespoons finely chopped fresh dill
- 6 cups fresh corn kernels (6 to 8 medium ears)
- 2 cups cherry tomatoes
- 4 yellow squash, cut into ½-inch pieces

1. Place all the ingredients into the insert of a 5- to 7-quart slow cooker. Cover with the lid and cook on high for 1½ to 2 hours, until the corn and tomatoes have softened.
2. Keep on the warm setting and serve directly from the slow cooker.

Feta Cheese and Pine Nut Barley-Stuffed Cabbage Rolls

Prep time: 20 minutes | Cook time: 6 to 8 hours | Serves 4

- 1 large head green cabbage, cored
- 1 tablespoon olive oil
- 1 large yellow onion, chopped
- 3 cups cooked pearl barley
- 3 ounces (85 g) feta cheese, crumbled
- ½ cup dried currants
- 2 tablespoons pine nuts, toasted
- 2 tablespoons chopped fresh flat-leaf parsley
- ½ teaspoon sea salt
- ½ teaspoon black pepper
- ½ cup apple juice
- 1 tablespoon apple cider vinegar
- 1 (15-ounce / 425-g) can crushed tomatoes, with the juice

1. Steam the cabbage head in a large pot over boiling water for 8 minutes. Remove to a cutting board and let cool slightly.
2. Remove 16 leaves from the cabbage head (reserve the rest of the cabbage for another use). Cut off the raised portion of the center vein of each cabbage leaf (do not cut out the vein).
3. Heat the oil in a large nonstick lidded skillet over medium heat. Add the onion, cover, and cook 6 minutes, or until tender. Remove to a large bowl.
4. Stir the barley, feta cheese, currants, pine nuts, and parsley into the onion mixture. Season with ¼ teaspoon of the salt and ¼ teaspoon of the pepper.
5. Place cabbage leaves on a work surface. On 1 cabbage leaf, spoon about ⅓ cup of the barley mixture into the center. Fold in the edges of the leaf over the barley mixture and roll the cabbage leaf up as if you were making a burrito. Repeat for the remaining 15 cabbage leaves and filling.
6. Arrange the cabbage rolls in the slow cooker.
7. Combine the remaining ¼ teaspoon salt, ¼ teaspoon pepper, the apple juice, apple cider vinegar, and tomatoes. Pour the apple juice mixture evenly over the cabbage rolls.
8. Cover and cook on high 2 hours or on low for 6 to 8 hours. Serve hot.

Parsley Smashed Potatoes

Prep time: 20 minutes | Cook time: 6 hours | Serves 8

- 16 small red potatoes
- 1 celery rib, sliced
- 1 medium carrot, sliced
- ¼ cup finely chopped onion
- 2 cups chicken broth
- 1 tablespoon minced fresh parsley
- 1½ teaspoons salt, divided
- 1 teaspoon pepper, divided
- 1 garlic clove, minced
- 2 tablespoons butter, melted
- Additional minced fresh parsley

1. Place the potatoes, celery, carrot, and onion in a 4-quart slow cooker. In a small bowl, whisk together the broth, parsley, 1 teaspoon salt, ½ teaspoon pepper, and garlic, then pour the mixture over the vegetables. Cover and cook on low for 6 to 8 hours, until the potatoes are tender.
2. Remove the potatoes from the slow cooker and transfer them to a 15x10x1-inch pan, discarding the cooking liquid and vegetables. Gently flatten the potatoes with the bottom of a measuring cup, then move them to a large bowl. Drizzle with butter, sprinkle with the remaining salt and pepper, and toss to coat. Finish with a garnish of extra parsley.

Sweet-Sour Cabbage

Prep time: 20 minutes | Cook time: 3 to 5 hours | Serves 6

- 1 medium head red or green cabbage, shredded
- 2 onions, chopped
- 4 tart apples, pared, quartered
- ½ cup raisins
- ¼ cup lemon juice
- ¼ cup cider, or apple juice
- 3 tablespoons honey
- 1 tablespoon caraway seeds
- ⅛ teaspoon allspice
- ½ teaspoon salt

1. Place all the ingredients into the slow cooker and stir to mix.
2. Cover and cook on high for 3 to 5 hours, adjusting the time based on whether you prefer the cabbage and onions more crisp or softer.

Brown Rice and Vegetable Pilaf

Prep time: 20 minutes | Cook time: 5 hours | Serves ¾ cup

- 1 onion, minced
- 1 cup sliced cremini mushrooms
- 2 carrots, sliced
- 2 garlic cloves, minced
- 1½ cups long grain brown rice
- 2½ cups vegetable broth
- ½ teaspoon salt
- ½ teaspoon dried marjoram leaves
- ⅛ teaspoon freshly ground black pepper
- ⅓ cup grated Parmesan cheese

1. Add the onion, mushrooms, carrots, garlic, and rice to the slow cooker.
2. Pour in the broth, season with salt, marjoram, and pepper, then stir to combine.
3. Cover with the lid and cook on low for about 5 hours, until the rice is tender and the liquid has been absorbed.
4. Stir in the cheese just before serving.

Extra Green Beans

Prep time: 15 minutes | Cook time: 1 to 2 hours | Serves 5

- 2 (14½-ounce / 411-g) cans green beans, undrained
- 1 cup cooked cubed ham
- ⅓ cup finely chopped onion
- 1 tablespoon butter, melted, or bacon drippings

1. Place undrained beans in cooker. Add remaining ingredients and mix well.
2. Cook on high 1 to 2 hours, or until steaming hot.

Bavarian-Style Cabbage

Prep time: 10 minutes | Cook time: 3 to 8 hours | Serves 4 to 8

- 1 small head red cabbage, sliced
- 1 medium onion, chopped
- 3 tart apples, cored and quartered
- 2 teaspoons salt
- 1 cup hot water
- 2 tablespoons sugar
- ⅓ cup vinegar
- 3 tablespoons bacon drippings

1. Place all ingredients in slow cooker in order listed.
2. Cover. Cook on low 8 hours, or on high 3 hours. Stir well before serving.

Chapter 10

Desserts

Chapter 10 Desserts

Butter and Sugar Slow-Simmered Soft Apples

Prep time: 20 minutes | Cook time: 2 to 2½ hours | Makes about 7 cups

- ¾ cup sugar
- 3 tablespoons flour
- 1½ teaspoons cinnamon (optional)
- 5 large baking apples, pared, cored, and diced into ¾-inch pieces
- Half a stick butter, melted
- 3 tablespoons water
- Nonstick cooking spray

1. Spray interior of slow cooker with nonstick cooking spray.
2. In a large bowl, mix sugar and flour together, along with cinnamon if you wish. Set aside.
3. Mix apples, butter, and water together in slow cooker. Gently stir in flour mixture until apples are well coated.
4. Cover and cook on high 1½ hours, and then on low 30 to 60 minutes, or until apples are done to your liking.
5. Serve.

Brownie Chocolate Cake

Prep time: 10 minutes | Cook time: 3 hours | Serves 12

- ½ cup plus 1 tablespoon unsalted butter, melted, divided
- 1½ cups almond flour
- ¾ cup cocoa powder
- ¾ cup granulated erythritol
- 1 teaspoon baking powder
- ¼ teaspoon fine salt
- 1 cup heavy (whipping) cream
- 3 eggs, beaten
- 2 teaspoons pure vanilla extract
- 1 cup whipped cream

1. Use 1 tablespoon of the melted butter to generously grease the slow-cooker insert.
2. In a large mixing bowl, stir together the almond flour, cocoa powder, erythritol, baking powder, and salt until everything is evenly distributed.
3. In another medium bowl, whisk the remaining ½ cup of melted butter with the heavy cream, eggs, and vanilla until smooth and well blended.
4. Slowly add the wet mixture into the bowl of dry ingredients, whisking until a uniform batter forms. Spoon this batter directly into the greased insert.
5. Place the lid on and cook on low for about 3 hours. Once finished, lift the insert out of the cooker and let the cake rest for 1 hour before serving.
6. Serve the cake warm, topping each portion with a generous dollop of whipped cream.

Crock-Baked Apples

Prep time: 15 minutes | Cook time: 2½ to 3 hours | Serves 8

- 8 medium apples
- ½ cup golden raisins
- ½ cup finely chopped walnuts
- 1 cup firmly packed light brown sugar
- 1 teaspoon ground cinnamon
- 2 tablespoons dark rum
- 4 tablespoons (½ stick) unsalted butter, melted and slightly cooled
- 1½ cups apple juice or apple cider
- Unsweetened whipped cream, for garnish
- Cinnamon sugar, for garnish

1. Core the apples and place them in the insert of a 5- to 7-quart slow cooker. In a mixing bowl, combine the raisins, walnuts, sugar, cinnamon, rum, and butter, then spoon the mixture into the apples. Pour the apple juice into the bottom of the insert. Cover with the lid and cook on low for 2½ to 3 hours, or on high until the apples are tender.
2. Carefully lift the apples out with a spatula, making sure to catch any filling that might spill from the bottoms.
3. Serve warm, topped with some of the cooking sauce and a dollop of whipped cream, then sprinkle lightly with cinnamon sugar.

Chocolate-Chile Cheesecake

Prep time: 15 minutes | Cook time: 2½ hours | Serves 8 to 10

Crust:

- 3 cups chocolate digestive biscuits (or chocolate graham crackers, or any plain chocolate cookies), crushed
- 1 tablespoon unsweetened cocoa powder
- ⅔ cup unsalted butter, melted

Filling:

- 1 pound (454 g) cream cheese
- ⅔ cup sour cream
- 3 large eggs, plus 3 egg yolks
- ¾ cup sugar
- 5 to 6 ounces (142 to 170 g) dark chocolate (you can use chili chocolate)
- ½ tablespoon unsweetened cocoa powder mixed with 1 tablespoon hot water
- 3 to 4 dried chiles, very finely crushed

Make the Crust:

1. Place a rack in the bottom of the slow cooker, or crumple foil into a zigzag shape so a cake pan can rest on top. Pour in about 1 cup of hot water.
2. Grease a 7-inch springform pan thoroughly.
3. Mix together the crushed biscuits, cocoa, and melted butter, pressing this mixture firmly into the bottom of the springform pan. Smooth the surface, then place the pan in the freezer for around 10 minutes.

Make the Filling:

4. In a large bowl, beat the cream cheese until smooth, then mix in the sour cream. Add the eggs and yolks, followed by the sugar, beating until everything is well combined.
5. Melt the chocolate using a double-boiler method: simmer water in a saucepan and set a glass bowl with the chocolate over it, making sure it doesn't touch the water. Stir until melted and smooth. (Alternatively, microwave the chocolate on high for 1 minute, then stir until fully melted.)
6. In a small bowl, stir the melted chocolate with the cocoa-and-water mixture, then add the crushed chiles and blend well. Fold this chile mixture into the cream mixture until smooth and even.
7. Remove the crust from the freezer and wrap the outside of the springform pan with foil. Pour the chocolate filling into the prepared crust.
8. Carefully place the pan on top of the rack or foil in the slow cooker, ensuring it doesn't touch the sides.
9. Set the slow cooker to high. Lay a kitchen towel over the top before placing the lid on, then cook for 2½ hours.
10. Turn off the cooker but leave it unopened; allow the cake to rest inside for 1 additional hour.
11. Take the pan out, remove the foil, and cool completely before refrigerating overnight.
12. Before serving, let the cake sit at room temperature for about 20 minutes, then release it from the pan. Slice and enjoy with a generous dollop of whipped cream.

Bread Pudding with Cappuccino

Prep time: 15 minutes | Cook time: 3 hours | Serves 8

- 8 cups torn stale egg bread, challah or croissants
- 2 cups chocolate chips or chopped chocolate
- 3 cups heavy cream
- 1 cup brewed espresso or strong coffee
- 8 large eggs
- 1 tablespoon vanilla extract
- 2 teaspoons ground cinnamon
- 1½ cups sugar
- ½ cup sugar mixed with 1 teaspoon ground cinnamon, for garnish (optional)
- Hot fudge sauce for drizzling (optional)

1. Spray the insert of a 5- to 7-quart slow cooker with nonstick cooking spray or line it with a slow-cooker liner according to the manufacturer's directions.
2. Spread the torn bread evenly in the bottom of the slow-cooker insert and sprinkle with the chocolate chips. Whisk together the cream, espresso, eggs, vanilla, cinnamon, and sugar in a large bowl until blended. Pour over the bread and chocolate, pushing the bread down to submerge it.
3. Sprinkle the pudding with the cinnamon sugar (if using). Cover the slow cooker and cook on high for about 3 hours, until puffed and an instant-read thermometer inserted in the center registers 185ºF (85ºC). Uncover and allow the pudding to cool for about 30 minutes.
4. Serve from the cooker set on warm and accompany with hot fudge sauce for drizzling.

Cranberry Applesauce with Chunks

Prep time: 15 minutes | Cook time: 3 to 4 hours | Serves 6

- 6 baking apple, peeled or unpeeled, cut into 1-inch cubes
- ½ cup apple juice
- ½ cup fresh or frozen cranberries
- ¼ cup sugar
- ¼ teaspoon ground cinnamon (optional)

1. Combine all ingredients in slow cooker.
2. Cover and cook on low 3 to 4 hours, or until apples are as soft as you like them.
3. Serve warm, or refrigerate and serve chilled.

Tiramisu Bread Pudding

Prep time: 15 minutes | Cook time: 3 hours | Serves 10

- ½ cup water
- ⅓ cup granulated sugar
- 1½ tablespoons instant espresso granules
- 2 tablespoons coffee-flavoured liqueur (like Kahlúa)
- 2 cups whole milk
- 2 large eggs, lightly beaten
- 8 ounces (227 g) French bread, cut into 1-inch cubes (about 8 cups)
- Nonstick cooking oil spray
- ⅓ cup Mascarpone cheese
- 1 teaspoon vanilla extract
- 2 teaspoons unsweetened cocoa powder

1. In a small saucepan over medium-high heat, combine the water, sugar, and espresso granules. Bring to a boil, letting it cook for 1 minute while stirring occasionally. Remove from the heat and stir in the liqueur.
2. In a large bowl, whisk together 1¾ cups of the milk and the eggs. Gradually whisk in the espresso mixture, then add the bread cubes and stir until they are well coated.
3. Spray a 2½-quart round baking dish with nonstick cooking oil spray. Pour the bread mixture into the dish and place it inside the slow cooker. Cover and cook on low for about 2 hours, or until set. Remove the dish, allow it to cool, and refrigerate for about 3 hours until chilled.
4. In a small bowl, whisk together the remaining ¼ cup milk, mascarpone cheese, and vanilla until smooth. Serve the chilled bread pudding topped with this mascarpone sauce and a light dusting of cocoa.

Apple-Pear Streusel

Prep time: 20 minutes | Cook time: 7 hours | Serves 2

- Nonstick cooking spray
- 4 apples, peeled and sliced
- 2 pears, peeled and sliced
- ¼ cup brown sugar
- 1 tablespoon freshly squeezed lemon juice
- ½ teaspoon ground cinnamon
- 2 tablespoons butter, plus 3 tablespoons cut into cubes, divided
- ½ cup light cream
- 1 cup all-purpose flour
- ½ cup rolled oats
- ½ cup chopped pecans
- ⅓ cup granulated sugar

1. Lightly coat the inside of the slow cooker with nonstick cooking spray.
2. Add the apple and pear slices to the cooker, then sprinkle with brown sugar, lemon juice, and cinnamon. Mix gently, dot the top with 2 tablespoons of butter, and pour the cream over the fruit.
3. In a medium bowl, stir together the flour, oats, pecans, and granulated sugar. Add the remaining 3 tablespoons of butter, cut into cubes, and work it in with two knives or a pastry blender until the mixture becomes crumbly. Scatter this topping evenly over the fruit.
4. Cover the slow cooker and cook on low for 7 hours, or until the fruit is soft and tender.

Southwestern-Style Cranberries

Prep time: 5 minutes | Cook time: 2 to 3 hours | Serves 8

- 1 (16-ounce / 454-g) can whole berry cranberry sauce
- 1 (10½-ounce / 298-g) jar jalapeño jelly
- 2 tablespoons chopped fresh cilantro

1. Combine ingredients in slow cooker.
2. Cover. Cook on low 2 to 3 hours.
3. Cool. Serve at room temperature.

Cornmeal Blueberry Buckle

Prep time: 25 minutes | Cook time: 3½ hours | Serves 6 to 8

- Nonstick baking spray

Batter:
- 1¼ cups all-purpose flour
- ¾ cup fine yellow cornmeal
- 1½ teaspoons baking powder
- ¼ teaspoon baking soda
- 2 teaspoon coarse salt
- ½ cup (1 stick) unsalted butter, room temperature
- 1 cup granulated sugar
- 2 teaspoon vanilla extract
- 2 large eggs
- ¾ cup buttermilk, preferably full-fat
- 1 cup blueberries

Streusel:
- ½ cup all-purpose flour
- 3 tablespoons light brown sugar
- 3 tablespoons unsalted butter, room temperature
- ½ teaspoon ground cinnamon

1. Lightly coat the insert of a 4-quart slow cooker with baking spray. Line bottom with parchment and spray.

Make the Batter:

2. Whisk together flour, cornmeal, baking powder, baking soda, and salt in a bowl. With an electric mixer on medium, beat butter, sugar, and vanilla until pale and fluffy, 3 to 5 minutes. Beat in eggs, one at a time. Add flour mixture in three batches, alternating with buttermilk; beat until combined.

3. Transfer batter to slow cooker; smooth top with an offset spatula. Top with blueberries. Wrap lid with a clean kitchen towel, gathering the ends at top (to absorb condensation). Cover and cook on high for 2 hours (or on low for 4 hours); cake will be undercooked. Rotate halfway through for even baking.

Make the Streusel:

4. In a small bowl, combine flour, brown sugar, butter, and cinnamon. Using a fork, mix butter into flour mixture until fine crumbs form. Using your hands, squeeze together the mixture to form large clumps.

5. Scatter streusel on top of cake, concentrating mixture around edges. Cover and cook on high until a tester inserted in center comes out clean, 1 to 1½ hours longer (or on low for 2 to 3 hours). Cool in pan for 15 minutes, then invert onto a cutting board; invert again onto a wire rack to cool completely, right side up.

Classic Rice Pudding

Prep time: 10 minutes | Cook time: 2½ to 3 hours | Serves 6 to 8

- 5 cups whole milk
- 2 cups heavy cream
- 1¼ cups sugar
- 1 teaspoon vanilla bean paste
- ½ teaspoon freshly grated nutmeg
- 1 cup Arborio or other medium-grain rice, rinsed several times with cold water and drained

1. Coat the insert of a 5- to 7-quart slow cooker with nonstick cooking spr ay. Whisk together the milk, cream, sugar, vanilla bean paste, and nutmeg in a large bowl and pour into the slow-cooker insert. Add the rice and stir to combine.

2. Cover and cook on low for 2½ to 3 hours, until the pudding is soft and creamy and the rice is tender. Remove the cover, turn off the cooker, and allow to cool for 30 minutes.

3. Serve warm, at room temperature, or chilled.

Almond Golden Cake

Prep time: 15 minutes | Cook time: 3 hours | Serves 8

- ½ cup coconut oil, divided
- 1½ cups almond flour
- ½ cup coconut flour
- ½ cup granulated erythritol
- 2 teaspoons baking powder
- 3 eggs
- ½ cup coconut milk
- 2 teaspoons pure vanilla extract
- ½ teaspoon almond extract

1. Line the insert of a 4-quart slow cooker with aluminum foil, then grease the foil with 1 tablespoon of coconut oil.

2. In a medium bowl, combine the almond flour, coconut flour, erythritol, and baking powder, mixing well.

3. In a separate large bowl, whisk together the remaining coconut oil, eggs, coconut milk, vanilla, and almond extract until smooth.

4. Add the dry mixture to the wet mixture, stirring until everything is fully blended.

5. Pour the batter into the prepared insert and smooth the surface with a spatula.

6. Cover the slow cooker and cook on low for about 3 hours, or until a toothpick inserted into the center comes out clean.

7. Lift the cake carefully from the insert, let it cool completely, and then serve.

Spiced Warm Gingerbread

Prep time: 10 minutes | Cook time: 3 hours | Serves 8

- 1 tablespoon coconut oil
- 2 cups almond flour
- ¾ cup granulated erythritol
- 2 tablespoons coconut flour
- 2 tablespoons ground ginger
- 2 teaspoons baking powder
- 2 teaspoons ground cinnamon
- ½ teaspoon ground nutmeg
- ¼ teaspoon ground cloves
- Pinch salt
- ¾ cup heavy (whipping) cream
- ½ cup butter, melted
- 4 eggs
- 1 teaspoon pure vanilla extract

1. Lightly grease the insert of the slow cooker with coconut oil.
2. In a large bowl, stir together the almond flour, erythritol, coconut flour, ginger, baking powder, cinnamon, nutmeg, cloves, and salt.
3. In a medium bowl, whisk together the heavy cream, butter, eggs, and vanilla.
4. Add the wet ingredients to the dry ingredients and stir to combine.
5. Spoon the batter into the insert.
6. Cover and cook on low for 3 hours, or until a toothpick inserted in the center comes out clean.
7. Serve warm.

Orange-Honey Cinnamon Slow-Cooked Apple Pudding Cake

Prep time: 15 minutes | Cook time: 2 hours | Serves 10

- 2 cups all-purpose flour
- ⅔ cup plus ¼ cup sugar, divided
- 3 teaspoons baking powder
- 1 teaspoon salt
- ½ cup cold butter
- 1 cup 2% milk
- 2 medium tart apples, peeled and chopped
- 1½ cups orange juice
- ½ cup honey
- 2 tablespoons butter, melted
- 1 teaspoon ground cinnamon
- 1⅓ cups sour cream
- ¼ cup confectioners' sugar

1. In a small bowl, combine the flour, ⅔ cup sugar, baking powder and salt. Cut in butter until mixture resembles coarse crumbs. Stir in milk just until moistened. Spread into the bottom of a greased 4- or 5-quart slow cooker; sprinkle apples over batter.
2. In a small bowl, combine the orange juice, honey, melted butter, cinnamon and remaining sugar; pour over apples. Cover and cook on high for 2 to 3 hours or until apples are tender.
3. In a small bowl, combine sour cream and confectioners' sugar. Serve with warm pudding cake.

Chocolate Hazelnut Bread Pudding

Prep time: 15 minutes | Cook time: 5 hours | Serves 8 to 10

- Nonstick cooking oil spray
- 14 ounces (397 g) challah bread, cut into 1-inch cubes (about 12 cups)
- ½ cup semisweet chocolate chips
- 2 cups heavy cream
- 2 cups whole milk
- 9 large egg yolks, room temperature
- 1 cup chocolate hazelnut spread (like Nutella)
- ¾ cup granulated sugar plus 1 tablespoon
- 4 teaspoons vanilla extract
- ¾ teaspoon salt
- 2 tablespoons light brown sugar

1. Line the insert of the slow cooker with aluminum foil and spray it lightly with nonstick cooking oil spray.
2. Position the oven rack in the center and preheat the oven to 225°F (107°C).
3. Spread the bread cubes on a baking sheet and bake for about 40 minutes, shaking the pan occasionally, until they are dry and crisp. Allow them to cool for 5 minutes before transferring to a very large bowl.
4. Stir the chocolate chips into the dried bread cubes, then pour the mixture into the prepared slow cooker.
5. In a large bowl, whisk together the cream, milk, egg yolks, chocolate hazelnut spread, ¾ cup sugar, vanilla, and salt. Pour this custard mixture evenly over the bread cubes in the cooker, pressing down gently to submerge the bread.
6. Combine the remaining 1 tablespoon granulated sugar with the brown sugar in a small bowl and sprinkle evenly over the top.
7. Cover and cook on low for about 4 hours, or until the center is set.
8. Let the pudding cool for 30 minutes. Lift it out of the slow cooker using the foil edges, transfer to a large shallow bowl, and serve either warm or chilled.

Very Vanilla Slow Cooker Cheesecake

Prep time: 40 minutes | Cook time: 2 hours | Serves 6

- ¾ cup graham cracker crumbs
- 1 tablespoon sugar plus ⅔ cup sugar, divided
- ¼ teaspoon ground cinnamon
- 2½ tablespoons butter, melted

Topping:
- 2 ounces (57 g) semisweet chocolate, chopped
- 2 (8-ounce / 227-g) packages cream cheese, softened
- ½ cup sour cream
- 2 to 3 teaspoons vanilla extract
- 2 eggs, lightly beaten
- 1 teaspoon shortening
- Toasted sliced almonds

1. Prepare a 6-inch springform pan by greasing it well, then set it on a double layer of heavy-duty foil (about 12 inches square). Wrap the foil securely around the outside of the pan.
2. Pour 1 inch of water into the bottom of a 6-quart slow cooker. Stack two 24-inch strips of foil, roll them lengthwise into a strip about 1 inch wide, and form a circle to act as a rack in the cooker.
3. In a small bowl, combine the cracker crumbs with 1 tablespoon of sugar and the cinnamon. Stir in the melted butter until evenly moistened, then press the mixture firmly into the bottom and about 1 inch up the sides of the springform pan.
4. Using a large mixing bowl, beat the cream cheese with the remaining sugar until smooth. Blend in the sour cream and vanilla. Add the eggs, mixing on low just until incorporated. Pour this filling into the prepared crust.
5. Carefully position the springform pan on top of the foil circle inside the slow cooker, making sure the pan doesn't touch the sides. Lay two layers of white paper towels across the top of the cooker, then secure the lid over them. Cook on high for 2 hours.
6. Once the cooking is done, turn off the heat but do not lift the lid. Leave the cheesecake inside the cooker for 1 additional hour to set.
7. Take the springform pan out of the cooker, remove the foil wrapping, and transfer to a wire rack. Let the cheesecake cool for 1 more hour, then run a knife around the edges to loosen. Cover and refrigerate overnight once fully cooled.
8. For the topping, microwave the chocolate and shortening together until melted and smooth, stirring to blend. Let it cool slightly, then remove the rim from the springform pan. Pour the chocolate mixture over the chilled cheesecake and finish with a sprinkle of almonds before serving.

Classic Pots de Crème

Prep time: 10 minutes | Cook time: 1½ to 2 hours | Serves 6 to 8

- 8 to 10 cups boiling water
- ¾ cup whole milk
- ¾ cup heavy cream
- 1 cup chopped semisweet chocolate
- 4 large egg yolks
- ⅓ cup sugar
- Unsweetened whipped cream for serving

1. Place a slow-cooker insert rack on the bottom of a 5- to 7-quart slow cooker and set out 6 (4-ounce / 113-g) ramekins.
2. Pour in enough of the boiling water to come halfway up the sides of the ramekins when they are eventually added to the cooker. Cover the cooker and set on high to keep the water hot.
3. Heat the milk and cream in a medium saucepan until small bubbles begin to form around the edges of the pan. Remove from the heat, add the chocolate, and stir until the chocolate is melted and the mixture is slightly cooled.
4. Whisk together the egg yolks and sugar in a mixing bowl, then whisk in the chocolate mixture. Strain the custard through a fine-mesh sieve into a large measuring cup. Pour the custard into the ramekins, cover each one with aluminum foil, and set on the rack in the slow cooker insert.
5. Cover and cook on high for 1½ to 2 hours, until set. They may be a bit jiggly in the middle but they will firm as they cool. Remove the foil, allow the custards to cool to room temperature, and refrigerate until chilled.
6. Serve the pots de crème with a dollop of whipped cream on top.

Sour Cream Amaretti Cheesecake

Prep time: 15 minutes | Cook time: 3 hours | Serves 6

- ¾ cup amaretti cookie crumbs (around 20 cookies, crushed)
- 2½ tablespoons unsalted butter, melted
- ½ teaspoon salt
- ¼ teaspoon ground cinnamon
- ⅓ cup granulated sugar, plus 1 tablespoon
- 12 ounces (340 g) cream cheese, at room temperature
- 1 tablespoon all-purpose flour
- 2 large eggs
- 1 teaspoon almond extract
- 1 cup sour cream

1. In a medium bowl, stir together the cookie crumbs, melted butter, ¼ teaspoon of the salt, cinnamon, and 1 tablespoon of sugar. Press this crumb mixture firmly into the bottom and about 1 inch up the side of a 6-inch springform pan to create the crust.
2. Using an electric mixer in another medium bowl, beat the cream cheese, flour, remaining ⅔ cup sugar, and the remaining ¼ teaspoon salt on medium-high speed until the mixture is smooth.
3. Scrape down the bowl, then add the eggs and almond extract, mixing until just blended.
4. Add the sour cream and continue beating until smooth and creamy.
5. Pour the prepared batter into the springform pan over the cookie crumb crust.
6. Pour ½ inch of water into the slow cooker and place a rack at the bottom, ensuring the top of the rack sits above the water. Set the cheesecake pan on the rack. Cover the cooker with a triple layer of paper towels, then secure the lid. Cook on high for 2 hours without lifting the lid.
7. After cooking, turn off the heat and let the cheesecake stand in the closed cooker for at least 1 more hour as it cools, again without removing the lid.
8. Take out the cheesecake and chill in the refrigerator for about 3 hours before slicing into wedges and serving.

Appendix 1

Measurement Conversion Chart

VOLUME EQUIVALENTS (DRY)

US STANDARD	METRIC (APPROXIMATE)
1/8 teaspoon	0.5 mL
1/4 teaspoon	1 mL
1/2 teaspoon	2 mL
3/4 teaspoon	4 mL
1 teaspoon	5 mL
1 tablespoon	15 mL
1/4 cup	59 mL
1/2 cup	118 mL
3/4 cup	177 mL
1 cup	235 mL
2 cups	475 mL
3 cups	700 mL
4 cups	1 L

WEIGHT EQUIVALENTS

US STANDARD	METRIC (APPROXIMATE)
1 ounce	28 g
2 ounces	57 g
5 ounces	142 g
10 ounces	284 g
15 ounces	425 g
16 ounces (1 pound)	455 g
1.5 pounds	680 g
2 pounds	907 g

VOLUME EQUIVALENTS (LIQUID)

US STANDARD	US STANDARD (OUNCES)	METRIC (APPROXIMATE)
2 tablespoons	1 fl.oz.	30 mL
1/4 cup	2 fl.oz.	60 mL
1/2 cup	4 fl.oz.	120 mL
1 cup	8 fl.oz.	240 mL
1 1/2 cup	12 fl.oz.	355 mL
2 cups or 1 pint	16 fl.oz.	475 mL
4 cups or 1 quart	32 fl.oz.	1 L
1 gallon	128 fl.oz.	4 L

TEMPERATURES EQUIVALENTS

FAHRENHEIT (F)	CELSIUS (C) (APPROXIMATE)
225 °F	107 °C
250 °F	120 °C
275 °F	135 °C
300 °F	150 °C
325 °F	160 °C
350 °F	180 °C
375 °F	190 °C
400 °F	205 °C
425 °F	220 °C
450 °F	235 °C
475 °F	245 °C
500 °F	260 °C

Appendix 2

Recipes Index

A

Acadiana Shrimp Barbecue	46
Almond Golden Cake	79
Apple Overnight Oatmeal	10
Apple-flavoured Stuffing	71
Apple-Pear Streusel	78
Artichoke Dip with Cream	67
Artichoke Party Bites	65
Auntie Ginny's Classic Baked Beans	15

B

Bacon Refried Beans	14
Bacon-and-Eggs Breakfast Casserole	5
Bacon-Pineapple Tater Tot Bake	64
Baked Beans with Pork Chops	33
Baked Tortilla Casserole	40
Baked-Style Oatmeal	7
Bandito Chili Dogs	39
Barbecued Lima Beans	13
Barbecued Party Starters	67
Barbecued Scallops and Shrimp with Spice	45
Barley Risotto with Shrimp and Artichokes	50
Bavarian-Style Cabbage	74
Bean Tator Tot Casserole	34
Beantown Scallops	50
Beef and Sausage Soup	54
Beef and Vegetable Soup	55
Beef Burgundy Stew	33
Beef Tongue	34
Bistro Chicken Thighs	27
Blueberry Delight	10
Braised Chicken Thighs with Garlic	24

Bread Pudding with Cappuccino	77
Breakfast Fruit Compote	6
Breakfast Risotto with Sausage	7
Breakfast Wassail	8
Broccoli and Cheese Soup	58
Broccoli Cornbread Bake	10
Brown Rice and Vegetable Pilaf	74
Brownie Chocolate Cake	76
Buffet Meat favourites	66
Butter and Sugar Slow-Simmered Soft Apples	76
Butter-Curried Crispy Almonds	64
Butterscotch Haystacks	63

C

Cajun Shrimp	46
Cajun-Style Beans with Sausage	15
Calico Beans with Bacon and Beef	13
Carrot Cake-Inspired Oatmeal	11
Carrots with Orange Thyme Glaze	71
Catalan Seafood Stew	48
Cheddar Cheese Rice	16
Cheesy Hash Browns	71
Chicken and Vegetable Medley	31
Chicken Azteca	30
Chicken Curry in Cream Sauce	27
Chicken Curry with Spice	26
Chicken Gumbo	25
Chicken in Coconut Curry	30
Chicken Stew Italian Style	24
Chicken with Mushrooms and Shallots	29
Chicken with Tropical Barbecue Sauce	27
Chili Boston Baked Beans	17
Chili con Carne	37

Chili Hot Dogs	34
Chocolate Hazelnut Bread Pudding	80
Chocolate Peanut Clusters	63
Chocolate-Chile Cheesecake	77
Cinco de Mayo Pork	37
Cioppino with Scallops and Crab	45
Classic Bouillabaisse	51
Classic Italian Slow-Simmered Meat Sauce Pasta	22
Classic Macaroni and Cheese	19
Classic Meat Loaf	34
Classic Pots de Crème	81
Classic Rice Pudding	79
Classic Wild Rice Pilaf	17
Coconut Butter Bread	5
Cod with Miso Glaze	43
Cola-Marinated Barbecue Steak	35
Corn and Shrimp Chowder	56
Cornbread from Scratch	11
Corned Beef and Cabbage with Fruit	37
Cornmeal Blueberry Buckle	79
Cottage Cheese Bread	10
Cottage Cheese Casserole	21
Crab Claws with Garlic	42
Crab Meat Soup	60
Cranberry Applesauce with Chunks	78
Creamy Broccoli Casserole	70
Creamy Corn and Potato Chowder	56
Creamy Tomato Soup	53
Creole Crayfish	47
Crock-Baked Apples	76
Cumin-Spiced Chicken Wings	24

D

| Double Cheese Cauliflower Soup | 56 |

E

Easy Baked Beans	13
Easy Beef Tortillas	36
Easy Spaghetti	21
Everyone's favourite Snack Mix	65

| Extra Green Beans | 74 |

F

Festive Cocktail Meatballs	37
Feta Cheese and Pine Nut Barley-Stuffed Cabbage Rolls	73
Fiery Curry Beef	35
From-Scratch Baked Beans	16
Fruited Wild Rice Pilaf	14

G

Garlic Potatoes	70
Garlic Swiss Fondue	68
Garlic Tilapia	49
German Potato Soup	61
Glazed Golden Carrots	72
Greek Shrimp Orzo	22
Green Beans Greek Style	72
Green Chili Chicken Stew	29
Gulf Shrimp Gumbo	44

H

Halibut with Lemon Garlic Butter	45
Hearty Lamb Stew	55
Hearty Meatball Stew	34
Herb-Braised Pork Chops	38
Herby Slow Cooker Kluski	20
Hot Bloody Mary Dip for Shrimp	67
Hot Crab Dip	65
Huevos Rancheros	7

I

| Indian Meatballs with Mint | 35 |
| Italian Roast with Potatoes | 33 |

J

| Joyce's Minestrone | 56 |

K

Kansas City Steak Soup	57
Karen's Classic Slow-Cooked Split Pea Soup	58
Kielbasa in Spicy Barbecue Sauce	64
Kielbasa with Apples	64

L

Lentil Sauce Pasta	21
Low Country Seafood Boil	50
Low-Calorie Soup	61

M

Mahi-Mahi with Tropical Fruit Salsa and Lentils	43
Mango Chutney Chicken	25
Mashed Sweet Potatoes with Garlic	70
Meatballs with Beef and Ham	39
Meat-Free Lasagna	20
Mediterranean Beef Pasta	19
Mediterranean Vegetable Stew	60
Miso Poached Salmon	49
Mixed Slow Cooker Beans	16

N

No-Meat Baked Beans	14

O

Oatmeal Bread and Raisin Stuffed Turkey Tenderloins	27
Oatmeal with Nuts	7
Old-Fashioned Beef and Barley Soup	54
One-Pot Chicken Supper	28
Orange-Glazed Chicken Breasts	26
Orange-Honey Cinnamon Slow-Cooked Apple Pudding Cake	80

Overnight Soaked Oatmeal	8

P

Pacifica Sweet-Hot Salmon	46
Parsley Smashed Potatoes	73
Pickled Whiting Fish	67
Poached Chicken Breasts	28
Poached Salmon Cakes in White Wine Butter Sauce	48
Poached Salmon of Provence	44
Polenta	9
Pork Roast with Cranberries	36
Pork with Lemon	36
Pot Roast Italiano	38
Potato-Crusted Sea Bass	47
Potatoes Baked in the Crock	72
Potatoes with Mustard	71
Pumpkin Black Bean Turkey Chili	28
Pumpkin Pecan N'Oatmeal Bowl	9
Pumpkin Pudding with Nutmeg	6

Q

Quick Beef Stew	60
Quick Broccoli Fix	72
Ranch-Style Beef	38
Reuben Chicken Casserole	25
Reuben Spread	63
Rice 'n Beans 'n Salsa	16
Rice and Turkey Slow Cooker Bake	15
Rich Honey-Glazed Smoked Little Sausages in Barbecue Sauce	66
Rich Low-Fat Slow-Cooker Beef Barbecue	36
Rich Vegetable Stock	60
Risi Bisi Pea and Rice	15
Roasted Tomato and Mozzarella Bruschetta	66
Rutabaga and Sweet Potato Garlic Soup	59

S

Salmon with Lemon Dijon and Dill Barley	44

Sausage and Hash-Brown Casserole	6
Sausage-Pasta Stew	59
savoury Butternut Squash and Apples	72
savoury Sesame-Infused Miso Soup with Tofu and Shrimp	53
Scandinavian-Style Beans	14
Sea Bass Tagine	47
Shrimp with Marinara Sauce	43
Sirloin steak	40
Slow Cooked Fruited Oatmeal with Nuts	10
Slow Cooker Kidney Beans	16
Slow-Cooked Meaty Jambalaya	13
Smoked Salmon and Potato Casserole	42
Snack Mix	63
Sour Cream Amaretti Cheesecake	82
South Indian Classic Tomato and Pepper Soup	57
South-of-the-Border Halibut	46
Southwest Breakfast Casserole	9
Southwestern Queso Dip	68
Southwestern-Style Cranberries	78
Spanakopita Frittata	11
Spiced Warm Gingerbread	80
Spicy Asian Braised Napa Cabbage Wraps	31
Spicy Jalapeno Spinach Dip	68
Spicy Rasta Wings	65
Spicy Taco Soup	55
Spicy Tomato Basil Mussels	42
Steak Soup	55
Strata with Salmon and Dill	8
Streusel Cake	5
Sweet and Sour Meatballs	64
Sweet Potato Dressing	70
Sweet Potato Lentil Stew	58
Sweet-Sour Cabbage	74
Swordfish with Citrus	48

T

Tarragon Chicken	28
Tender Halibut with Tangy Eggplant Ginger Relish	51
Tender Turkey Breast	29
Thai Peanut Wings	26
Thanksgiving Turkey Breast	25
Tiramisu Bread Pudding	78
Tomato, Corn, and Yellow Squash with Dill Butter	73
Traditional Beef Stew	58
Traditional Coconut Seafood Laksa	49
Tuna Noodle Casserole	20
Turkey in Tomato Braise	29
Turkey Minestrone	59

V

Vegetable Omelet	8
Vegetable Stew with Curry	53
Vegetarian Chili in Slow Cooker	17
Very Vanilla Slow Cooker Cheesecake	81
Vietnamese Beef and Noodle Soup	54

W

Warm Clam Dip	66
Warm Wheat Berry Cereal	9
Warming Spiced Butternut Squash Soup with Coconut Cream	57

Printed in Dunstable, United Kingdom